The LATEST Craze

A SHORT HISTORY of Mass Hysterias

JEFF FLEISCHER

© 2011 by Quirk Packaging, Inc.

This 2011 edition published by Fall River Press,
by arrangement with Quirk Packaging, Inc.

Design by Lynne Yeamans and Nancy Leonard

Fall River Press
122 Fifth Avenue
New York, NY 10011

ISBN: 978-1-4351-2977-1

Front cover art credits: Flying saucer © Art Parts; tulip © Dover Publications, Inc.;
shark © Dorling_Kindersley/iStockphoto

Printed and bound in Singapore

10   9   8   7   6   5   4   3   2   1

Contents

Introduction

"CRAZE" IS A PRETTY USEFUL, MULTI-PURPOSE WORD. It can mean a widespread fad or style, or it can just as easily mean a form of insanity or mania. In this book, it means all those things.

The crazes, manias, fads, trends and panics that make up the sixty-four stories in this book are all unique. They include panics that destroyed the whole world's economy and fears about the whole world getting destroyed. Trends encouraging kids to read and panics about them getting abused by Satan worshippers. Mysterious criminals terrorizing unsuspecting citizens and hideous clothing styles terrorizing good taste. They range from the harmless or even positive to the paranoid and destructive.

For all that variety, the crazes all share one important (and all too common) trait. An idea caught on, others noticed and, for good or ill, some form of chaos ensued.

Nowhere is that more true than the financial panics. All the bubbles followed the same general pattern—new idea, too much speculation, prices go up, prices go up too high, prices fall down and go boom. The evidence of past disasters was there for anyone to see, but people still got caught up in the mania, thinking *this time* everything would be different. In the details, yes. In the outcome, not so much.

That's not to say money is the only motivator for a craze. Just check out the mass hysterias. Weird or unexplained, real or imagined, some threat captured the public's attention and scared a lot more people than were ever actually in danger. Or the moral panics, where concerned parents, Puritanical busybodies or even official types got some menacing idea in their heads—that their neighbors were in league with the devil, that Communists were hiding under their bed, that a book/album/game was going to turn everyone into sex-and-violence-crazed maniacs—and tried to enforce that idea on everybody.

The same hive mind comes up a lot in fashion trends and in pop culture in general, where hype or peer pressure can help an idea go from obscure to mainstream to played out in a short time, or create a trend that stays relevant for years or decades. And as modern technology and improved knowledge change the world at a faster pace, there are more chances for technological trends to cause problems, or for unnerving ideas about the future or the universe to drive beyond-our-control panics.

So check out all the latest crazes in *The Latest Craze* and do yourself a favor. Keep them in mind before you invest too much time or money in the next "can't-miss" trend. Because in the long run, most of them eventually miss.

Chapter 1

Financial Panics, Bubbles, and Crashes

PEOPLE JUST LOVE THE IDEA OF TRYING TO MAKE A QUICK BUCK, NO MATTER HOW MUCH THE IDEA SEEMS TOO GOOD TO BE TRUE. (Quick tip—it's *almost always* too good to be true.) Over the years, speculators and investors have bought into anything from untested Internet businesses to more railroads than a country could handle to flowers they thought would double in value. The lucky ones managed to get out early enough to make serious cash; others stayed in too long and learned the cardinal rule of speculation bubbles (and gravity): What goes up will eventually come down.

Tulipomania

Location: *The Netherlands* | Time Frame: *1630s*

WHILE NOW CLICHÉD DUTCH ICONS ALONG WITH WINDMILLS AND WOODEN CLOGS, TULIPS WEREN'T INTRODUCED TO THE NETHERLANDS UNTIL A FEW CENTURIES AGO. AND THE ECONOMIC HAVOC THEY CAUSED MADE MANY PEOPLE WISH THEY'D NEVER SEEN ONE.

Tulips originated in the Middle East, but in the late 1500s, they made their way to Holland, where the colorful, bulb-shaped flowers seemed truly exotic. The tulips also arrived at the exact right time. The Dutch Republic had just obtained freedom from Spain in 1581—paving the way for the "Dutch Golden Age"—and the young nation was dominating trade, both with Asia and with other European countries. That wealth created a newly moneyed class that was looking to trade disposable income for status.

> ✸
>
> ODDLY, THE POPULARITY OF TULIPS SKYROCKETED RIGHT AFTER MANY OF THE FLOWERS GOT HIT WITH A NEAR-FATAL VIRUS THAT DAMAGED BULBS BY MAKING THEM GROW FLOWERS WITH SPECTACULAR LINES, PATTERNS, AND COLORS, WHICH FETCHED HIGHER PRICES.
>
> ✸

THE RISE OF THE TULIP MARKET The life cycle of tulips—bulbs take a minimum of seven years to grow from seeds, and last only a few years once grown—helped keep supply low, and therefore, demand high. For a few decades, tulips sold with high prices but a reasonably stable trade. One man's luxury item inevitably becomes another man's way to make a buck, and speculators who saw the high price of tulips wanted in. Before long, a futures market developed, with traders signing contracts to buy tulips at the end of the season. A combination of these factors morphed the tulip trade into Tulipomania, with Dutch towns trading them on their exchanges, traders meeting en masse in bars, prices going haywire—and a speculative bubble inflating quickly during the 1630s.

The records that exist show a ridiculous rise in tulip prices starting in November 1636, with tulips selling for up to twenty times their original value in as little as one month. Speculators kept buying bulbs, assuming they could sell them as prices kept climbing, and soon people were trading their homes, land, or life savings for a single flower.

THE TULIP CRASH The market seemed like it would keep rising—until, at a Haarlem bulb auction in early 1637, traders were shocked to find nobody who was willing to buy. With the sudden realization that prices had peaked and it was probably time to get out, they

> ✻
>
> IN ONE EXAMPLE, A *SINGLE* TULIP BULB SOLD FOR: TWO LASTS OF WHEAT, FOUR LASTS OF RYE, FOUR OXEN, EIGHT PIGS, TWELVE SHEEP, 126 GALLONS OF WINE, FOUR CASKS OF BEER, TWO TONS OF BUTTER, A THOUSAND POUNDS OF CHEESE, A BED, A MAN'S SUIT, AND A SILVER CUP.
>
> ✻

started selling their bulbs at a loss, causing tulip prices to fall even faster than they'd risen. Some bulbs sold for a hundredth of what they had been worth a few weeks earlier. Many investors lost all their money, though intervention by the Dutch government limited the bubble's impact on the nontulip portion of the economy. The world had experienced its first major speculation bubble, the lessons of which investors would ignore for generations to come.

South Sea Bubble

LOCATION: *Great Britain* | TIME FRAME: *1720*

PERHAPS NO SINGLE STOCK IN HISTORY BETTER DEMONSTRATES THE ROLLER-COASTER NATURE OF THE MARKET THAN THAT OF THE SOUTH SEA COMPANY, ARGUABLY THE WORST STOCK TIP EVER.

The South Sea Company was started in 1711 and, as part of the Treaty of Utrecht ending the War of the Spanish Succession in 1713, got exclusive trading rights to all Spain's colonies in South America. (With a big catch—but more on that later.)

Before it even started to trade, however, the company got involved in financing public debt. Big-time. The British government, which had borrowed millions for the aforementioned war, convinced holders of its debt to trade that debt for shares in the South Sea Company. Because the government also guaranteed the company annual money in exchange for helping it out, the South Sea Company's new stockholders were seeing money even before there was

---

⚘✳⚘

BEFORE YOU FEEL TOO BAD FOR SOUTH SEA INVESTORS, CONSIDER THAT ONE OF THE MAIN "GOODS" THE COMPANY SENT TO THE COLONIES WAS PEOPLE. PART OF THE TRADING RIGHTS IT ACQUIRED WAS THE CONTRACT TO SUPPLY SLAVES TO SOUTH AMERICA, WHICH IT CONTINUED TO DO AFTER THE BUBBLE BURST.

---

actual South Sea trade. The company just kept buying government debt with more of its easily tradable shares.

WHY THE CRASH? Investors were eager, especially when company officials (fraudulently) talked up their stock's value, claiming the South American trade would bring back untold fortunes—even after early trade trips (starting in 1717) returned little profit, and even though the company could only send *one* trading ship a year under the terms of the treaty. The stock price took off. Shares worth £128 in January 1720 were worth £550 by the end of May. Smart investors knew this was nuts, and those who sold made out great. Others, ignoring that this stock was still based on a *potential* profit, kept buying.

THE MANIA CREATED BY SOUTH SEA STOCK DROVE INVESTMENT IN OTHER TRADING COMPANIES, WITH OFTEN SPECIOUS GOALS. EXAMPLES RANGED FROM A COMPANY "FOR IMPROVING THE ART OF MAKING SOAP" OR "FOR A WHEEL OF PERPETUAL MOTION" TO THE TEMPTINGLY VAGUE "FOR CARRYING ON AN UNDERTAKING OF GREAT ADVANTAGE; BUT NOBODY TO KNOW WHAT IT IS."

In August, the stock hit a ridiculous £1,000 per share—and it was all downhill from there. Scared investors started selling like crazy. Others who had "bought" their shares with loans from the company itself realized they couldn't afford the price and had to sell. By the following August, shares traded for less than £150, bankrupting thousands of shareholders and hurting the British economy as a whole. The bubble's bursting set off a 1721 investigation into fraud within the company. Some of the company's directors were arrested or had their estates seized, with some of the money going to bilked investors. The South Sea Company itself was broken up, but the restructured version continued to operate into the nineteenth century.

Panic of 1819

LOCATION: *United States* | TIME FRAME: *1819*

WHEN YOU'RE LIVING IN A TIME CALLED THE ERA OF GOOD FEELINGS, THE HUBRIS ALONE MAKES THE OTHER SHOE DROPPING SEEM ALMOST INEVITABLE. THE PANIC OF 1819 WAS THAT OTHER SHOE.

There was plenty of blame to go around. Much of it goes to the American banking system, which could be generously described as disorganized. The First National Bank's charter had expired in 1811, so when it came time to pay for the War of 1812, the federal government had to borrow from a bunch of state banks. With no Federal Reserve, individual banks were able to just print money at will to cover the loans (which they did) and thereby cause severe inflation.

Congress's 1816 creation of the Second Bank of the United States was in theory to create a strong, national, gold-backed currency. In practice, it wound up loaning money to the aforementioned print-happy banks to cover *their* debts. With their debts covered, the state banks just expanded and issued even more

---

CONTRARY TO POPULAR BELIEF, THE PANIC OF 1819 WASN'T AMERICA'S FIRST FINANCIAL CRISIS—TWO DOWNTURNS IN THE LATE 1700S SERIOUSLY IMPACTED THE UNITED STATES AS WELL AS OTHER NATIONS. BUT IT WAS THE FIRST ONE AMERICA GOT INTO ALL BY ITSELF—A DUBIOUS MILESTONE FOR A YOUNG AND GROWING NATION—AND ITS FIRST MAJOR DEPRESSION.

---

credit. In short, they started funding bubbles—in real estate, in construction, in transit. All of which helped the country modernize, but it was only a matter of time until the bills literally came due.

> THE SECOND BANK OUTLIVED THE PANIC, BUT FOUND A FIERCE ENEMY IN ANDREW JACKSON. AS PRESIDENT, IN 1832, HE VETOED CONGRESS'S ATTEMPT TO RECHARTER IT AND THEN WITHDREW ALL FEDERAL FUNDS FROM IT, CAUSING ITS COLLAPSE.

WHY THE CRASH? That started in 1818, when the national bank— which wisely saw the growth in speculation as unsustainable—began calling in some of its loans to smaller banks. Many couldn't come up with the cash and simply failed. Around the same time, the overseas trade that had been so profitable in the previous few years slowed dramatically, as the end of the Napoleonic Wars meant European farmers started producing again and their countries didn't need to import so much food. The big blow came in January 1819, when prices for cotton—the South's main cash crop— completely crashed as British investors started importing from India instead.

With banks failing, foreclosures became common, unemployment shot up, and investments dried up. More than a thousand people in Philadelphia alone were sent to debtors' prisons, and an estimated third of Americans were seriously affected. By 1823, the panic ended after five awful years. The federal bank had succeeded in getting inflation under control, and government relief efforts had helped broke landowners return their properties to the government for credit against their debts, while extending their credit so they could use it when the economy picked up. Things soon stabilized financially, and the country had a blueprint for how easily everything could go wrong.

Panic of 1837

LOCATION: *United States* | TIME FRAME: *1837*

POOR MARTIN VAN BUREN. AMERICA'S EIGHTH PRESIDENT HAD BARELY UNPACKED HIS BAGS AFTER MOVING INTO THE WHITE HOUSE WHEN A MASSIVE BANKING CRISIS SWEPT THE COUNTRY. FIVE WEEKS INTO THE JOB, HE'D NEVER GET A CHANCE TO SETTLE IN.

Of course, the collapse was set in motion well before Van Buren became president. Part of the irony is that in 1835, the federal government had nearly paid off the national debt in full—one of President Andrew Jackson's top goals—and the Treasury was running a significant surplus. Jackson's many vicious campaigns to drive Native Americans west had also opened up a ton of land for the federal government to sell to land speculators. Sounds great for the (non-Native) American economy, right?

"IF CONGRESS HAS THE RIGHT UNDER THE CONSTITUTION TO ISSUE PAPER MONEY," JACKSON ARGUED IN ONE ANTIGREEN-BACK RANT, "IT WAS GIVEN TO BE USED BY THEMSELVES, NOT TO BE DELEGATED TO INDIVIDUALS OR CORPORATIONS." BY WHICH HE MOSTLY MEANT BANKS.

Well, Jackson was worried about paper money, and the risk that inflation would render all those newly wide-open spaces bad investments if land prices fell. So worried that on his way out of office (in July 1836) he issued an executive order called the Specie Circular, which mandated that after August 5 government land could only be paid for with gold or silver "specie" coins (there was an exception for genuine homeowners, but even that expired in December). The problem, of course, was that most people buying land didn't have enough gold and silver sitting around and—with paper money now badly devalued thanks to the Circular—banks decided to hoard their metal rather than loan it out.

WHY THE CRASH? The speculation bubble was already starting to burst, and it did so for good on May 10, 1837, when every bank in New York City totally suspended payment in gold and silver. Banks not loaning money scared people, cued the bank runs, and started a depression. With paper money—which is what most people had—rendered nearly worthless, businesses took a huge hit. Bank failures in New York topped $100 million (in 1837 money, mind you) in just two months. By fall, roughly a third of all workers were unemployed and those who had jobs were seeing pay cuts as high as 50 percent. Homelessness went way up. At least 343 banks failed completely. Things were really bad, and they stayed bad. While there were brief signs of hope along the way, the depression didn't truly end until 1843.

> ❀
>
> JACKSON'S SPECIE CIRCULAR CREATED A MAJOR RIFT IN THE PRESIDENT'S PARTY—IT WAS THE KEY ISSUE IN JOHN BELL'S (FAILED) ATTEMPT TO REGAIN HIS JOB AS SPEAKER OF THE HOUSE FROM FUTURE PRESIDENT JAMES K. POLK AND IN BELL'S (AND OTHERS') DEFECTION FROM THE DEMOCRATS TO THE WHIGS.
>
> ❀

Railway Mania

IN 1840S GREAT BRITAIN, RAILROADS SEEMED LIKE A GREAT WAY TO MAKE MONEY. THAT IS, UNTIL TOO MANY PEOPLE HAD THE SAME IDEA AND, INEVITABLY, LOTS OF INVESTORS FOUND THEMSELVES RAILROADED.

Unlike some earlier financial manias, the railroad craze actually relied on an educated, successful populace. The British middle class had grown considerably thanks to the industrial revolution, and had money to invest. When the Bank of England cut interest rates in the mid-1840s, investors started looking for an alternative to low-interest government bonds, and railroads seemed like a good one.

Railroads *were* a good idea at the time, but only up to a point. The first modern intercity rail line had connected Liverpool and Manchester in 1830, and worked well. In the forties, a rash of prospective companies started proposing new routes and looking for money to build them. It's worth noting that by 1825, the British government had repealed the Bubble Act (which was passed after the South Sea Bubble burst, to avoid a situation just like this one), claiming it was no longer needed. Predictable results followed.

EVEN REALLY SMART PEOPLE GOT CAUGHT UP IN THE RAILWAY MANIA—INVESTORS INCLUDED CHARLES DARWIN, THE BRONTË SISTERS, CHARLES BABBAGE, AND JOHN STUART MILL.

Would-be railroad companies needed parliamentary help; they had to submit bills for the right to buy land and to have their proposed routes approved. But Parliament didn't really consider project viability, basically approving anything that wasn't intentionally misleading. During the peak of the railroad mania, a total of 272 Acts of Parliament authorizing railroad speculation passed—covering more than nine thousand miles of routes.

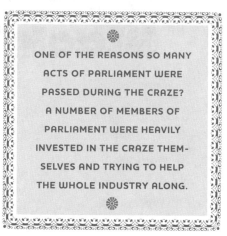

ONE OF THE REASONS SO MANY ACTS OF PARLIAMENT WERE PASSED DURING THE CRAZE? A NUMBER OF MEMBERS OF PARLIAMENT WERE HEAVILY INVESTED IN THE CRAZE THEMSELVES AND TRYING TO HELP THE WHOLE INDUSTRY ALONG.

WHY THE CRASH? Authorization made railroad companies look legit, and the companies advertised widely in respected newspapers, with claims that the needed rail lines were guaranteed moneymakers. Investors needed only a 10 percent deposit to buy shares, though the company could ask for the rest at any point. Those who could only afford the deposit—thinking they'd make enough that they wouldn't have to worry—were unpleasantly surprised when struggling lines demanded the rest, and many lost their savings as a result. Funding problems and incompetent proposals ensured that about a third of all proposed lines failed completely, while other projects were simply bought up at a discount by bigger rail companies.

While lots of people lost lots of money, the whole thing wasn't a waste. The rampant speculation did fund most of the British rail system. The projects authorized during the peak of the mania (1844–1846) wound up building more than six thousand miles of railways—more than half of today's total.

Black Friday

LOCATION: *United States* | TIME FRAME: *1869*

AS A COMMANDER OF UNION FORCES IN THE CIVIL WAR, ULYSSES S. GRANT WAS A GREAT GENERAL. AS PRESIDENT, WELL, HE WAS A GREAT GENERAL. THAT MADE HIS SCANDAL-RACKED ADMINISTRATION AN IDEAL TARGET FOR A PAIR OF SHYSTER SPECULATORS.

Jay Gould and Jim Fisk had previously teamed up in a successful 1868 effort to block Cornelius Vanderbilt from taking over their Erie Railroad. Of course, they (along with longtime Vanderbilt rival Daniel Drew) did this by letting Vanderbilt buy more shares, then just issuing more and more stock so he couldn't obtain a majority share and was forced to pull out at a huge loss, leaving them in control. For their next trick, they decided to corner the American gold market.

For their plan to work, they needed the White House to change its economic policy. Like his predecessor, Andrew Johnson, Grant had the treasury use gold in order to buy back greenback dollars in an attempt to get the greenbacks out of circulation. If the government instead kept its gold, and they bought up as much other gold as possible, Gould and Fisk could sell high and make a killing. So they

> WHILE FISK ESCAPED FINANCIAL RUIN, HE JUST COULDN'T STAY OUT OF TROUBLE. IN 1872, HE GOT HIMSELF SHOT DEAD IN AN ARGUMENT OVER MONEY AND A SHOWGIRL.

figured they would take advantage of Grant's tendency toward nepotism and his susceptibility to a con.

The pair enlisted the help of Abel Corbin, Grant's brother-in-law and himself a speculator. Corbin got the disreputable duo invited to events with the president, where they and Corbin would get into "spontaneous" discussions of why the government shouldn't sell gold. Corbin also convinced Grant to appoint

CORBIN WASN'T THE ONLY BROTHER-IN-LAW OF GRANT'S TO GET HIM IN HOT WATER. GRANT APPOINTED HIS SISTER'S HUSBAND, JAMES F. CASEY, COLLECTOR OF THE PORT OF NEW ORLEANS—WHERE HE ILLEGALLY SKIMMED MONEY. IN HIS JOB AS A WHITE HOUSE USHER, FREDERICK DENT (GRANT'S OTHER SISTER'S HUSBAND) OVERHEARD INSIDE INFORMATION AND RAN A SIDE BUSINESS SELLING THAT INFO.

Daniel Butterfield assistant treasurer of the United States—leaving out the fact that Butterfield was in on the scam, and promised to tip Gould and Fisk off if the government started selling.

WHY THE CRASH? On September 20, 1869, Gould and Fisk started buying as much gold as they could get their hands on, and the price of gold increased 30 percent from what it was when Grant took office earlier that year. What they hadn't expected was the president getting hip that something was up. On Friday, September 24, Grant had the government sell off $4 million in gold. Prices crashed in a matter of minutes, and a market panic saw even honest investors rushing to sell off their gold. It took years before the country recovered from the deflation caused by that day of gold-dumping panic. As for Gould and Fisk, they managed to sell before hitting bottom, though Corbin lost a fortune.

Panic of 1893

LOCATION: *United States* | TIME FRAME: *1893*

UNTIL THE GREAT DEPRESSION HIT, THE PANIC OF 1893 WAS CLEARLY THE WORST NATIONWIDE FINANCIAL DISASTER THE UNITED STATES HAD SEEN. AND BOY, DID IT SUCK.

America had already seen its share (actually, more than its share) of speculation bubbles, but it saw complete collapses in several parts of the country's economy in 1893. Historians generally date the start of the panic as February 23, the day the Philadelphia and Reading Railroad went bankrupt, but the railroad industry had been laying track for a collapse for a while. Speculation in railroads had built a huge bubble in the 1880s that followed the bubble blueprint—over-expansion, growth based on speculation, then collapse.

THE PANIC DID CREATE A POLITICAL STAR IN WILLIAM JENNINGS BRYAN. ONE OF THE GREAT PUBLIC SPEAKERS IN AMERICAN HISTORY, THE POPULIST LAWYER BECAME FAMOUS FOR HIS CRITIQUES OF THE GOVERNMENT'S HANDLING OF THE CRISIS AND IN 1896 BECAME (AT THIRTY-SIX) THE YOUNGEST MAN TO WIN A MAJOR PARTY'S NOMINATION FOR PRESIDENT.

WHY THE CRASH? The Reading collapse sparked a bunch of bank runs. Banks failed, causing businesses that needed money to fail. In total, five hundred banks collapsed during the panic, which helped fold more than fifteen thousand companies and drove up to one-fifth of the working population into unemployment. The collapse in wages prompted waves of strikes by industrial workers, most notably the July 1894 Pullman Strike that shut down most of America's railroads. Silver mines closed in serious numbers, many of them permanently.

If all that wasn't bad enough, there were the farms. Between 1870 and 1890, the number of farms in the United States had gone up almost 80 percent, with most of the new farmers holding mortgages. So when the banks started collapsing—and when a badly timed recession in Europe destroyed export prices—indebted farmers couldn't pay and started losing their land.

> IN A SORT OF REVERSE BAILOUT, NEW YORK BANKER JOHN PIERPONT MORGAN LOANED $65 MILLION IN GOLD TO THE FEDERAL GOVERNMENT AT THE HEIGHT OF THE PANIC, A MOVE THAT PROBABLY SAVED THE COUNTRY FROM BANKRUPTCY.

Oh, there was also the disastrous 1890 Sherman Silver Purchase Act, which required the federal government to buy a set amount of silver every year—and led to savvy citizens trading their silver for gold, rapidly depleting the government's gold supply. Oops.

In short, anything that could go wrong did, and the panic lasted four years. Things finally got better in 1897, largely thanks to an amazingly lucky strike. In August 1896, a small party found gold in Alaska, prompting the Klondike Gold Rush. It helped save the U.S. economy, which grew for a solid decade—before yet another financial panic hit in 1907.

Stock Market Crash

LOCATION: *Global* | TIME FRAME: *1929*

SURE, OTHER FINANCIAL PANICS WERE HORRIBLE IN THEIR OWN RIGHT. WHEN IT CAME TO COMPLETELY DESTROYING THE WORLD ECONOMY, HOWEVER, NOTHING DID QUITE AS GREAT OF A JOB AS THE GREAT DEPRESSION.

> BEFORE THE 1929 CRASH, THE TERM "GREAT DEPRESSION" WAS MOST OFTEN APPLIED TO VICTORIAN ENGLAND'S FINANCIAL TROUBLES FROM 1873 TO 1896. THAT CHANGED IN A HURRY, AS THIS CRASH SURPASSED THE EARLIER ONE, AND THE EARLIER ERA GOT RE-NICKNAMED THE "LONG DEPRESSION."

On the surface, the postwar "Roaring Twenties" looked like a time of prosperity in the United States. In reality, all the signs of a coming crisis were already in place. The stock market's value was high—partly because many thousands of Americans were investing with borrowed money. The country's wealth had gotten dangerously top-heavy, with the good fortunes of the rich making the economy look better in theory than it was in practice for most Americans. With the stock market seen as driving wealth, investors did what they did during every doomed bubble and just kept buying.

The market had quintupled in value in the six years before the crash, with a Dow Jones peak at 381.17 on September 3, before starting to tick back down. A day of reckoning was imminent. October 24 proved to be that day, as the market plummeted in a hurry, with a then-record 12.9 million shares being traded on "Black Thursday." Hoping to stop the panic, several of Wall Street's biggest-name bankers got together and started buying blue-chip stocks for more than they were selling at, starting with U.S. Steel. This tactic worked to a point, as prices stopped falling—temporarily. Within a week, however, the situation deteriorated.

THE PINNACLE Just five days later, "Black Thursday" looked like the good old days. On Tuesday, October 29, the market *really* fell apart, with roughly 16 million shares trading and the Dow falling to 230.07. The market lost $14 billion in one day, and $30 billion in a week. The Dow would actually get worse that November, but "Black Tuesday" was the economic shot heard round the world. Economists still debate whether the crash started the Depression or was merely a signal that it had arrived, but either way, life was about to get far more difficult all over the world.

WITH ITS POST–COMMUNIST REVOLUTION ISOLATION FROM THE WORLD ECONOMY, THE SOVIET UNION ACTUALLY AVOIDED MOST OF THE INITIAL EFFECTS OF THE STOCK MARKET CRASH. THE RISE OF FASCISM IN GERMANY, HOWEVER, WAS MUCH WORSE FOR THE SOVIETS THAN ANY FINANCIAL CRISIS, AS NO COUNTRY SUFFERED MORE CASUALTIES OR PROPERTY DESTRUCTION DURING WORLD WAR II.

In the United States alone, some 13 million people lost their jobs, as the unemployment rate went from 3 percent to 25 percent in a matter of months. With everyone broke, home building fell 80 percent between the crash and 1932. In 1933, many of America's farms were wiped out as the "Dust Bowl," a deadly combo of drought and erosion, left much of the Great Plains barren and forced farmers to head west looking for underemployment as migrant workers. In the early thirties, there were more Americans fleeing the country than there were immigrants coming in. Nine million people lost their entire savings. "Hoovervilles"—makeshift shantytowns named for President Herbert Hoover and his hands-off approach to the economy—became a common sight. By 1933, six of every ten Americans were living below the poverty line.

The situation wasn't any better overseas, as the Depression got exported to market economies all around the world almost immediately. British unemployment more than doubled by the end of 1930, while poverty in France prompted riots and attempts to overthrow the government. In Germany, conditions deteriorated rapidly. By 1932, unemployment there had hit 30 percent and a desperate public began to embrace extremism, paving the way for Adolf Hitler and the Nazis to take power in 1933, and setting the stage for the Second World War.

⇥✳⇤

THE DUST BOWL DID INSPIRE SOME OF THE GREAT AMERICAN ART OF THE ERA, INCLUDING JOHN STEINBECK'S NOVELS *THE GRAPES OF WRATH* AND *OF MICE AND MEN*, FOLKSINGER WOODY GUTHRIE'S *DUST BOWL BALLADS*, AND DOROTHEA LANGE'S ICONIC *MIGRANT MOTHER* AND OTHER BLACK-AND-WHITE PHOTOS.

THE AFTERMATH Things didn't start turning around in America until 1933, when new president Franklin D. Roosevelt introduced the first phases of his New Deal. The aggressive government package included dozens of new programs, and FDR continually scrapped those that weren't working and added to those that were. Highlights included the introduction of Social Security, the creation of jobs programs to fix infrastructure, a federal theater project for out-of-work actors, farm regulations that cut production in order to get prices back up, minimum wages, and improved labor standards. It was an unprecedented effort, and it worked. By 1936, most of the country's economic indicators were back to late 1920s levels—except unemployment, and even that had been halved.

HOOVERVILLES WEREN'T THE ONLY SIGNS OF POVERTY NICKNAMED FOR THE INEFFECTUAL PRESIDENT. THERE WERE ALSO "HOOVER BLANKETS" (OLD NEWSPAPERS), "HOOVER FLAGS" (EMPTY POCKETS TURNED INSIDE OUT), "HOOVER WAGONS" (CARS PULLED BY HORSES), AND "HOOVER LEATHER" (SHOE SOLES MADE OF CARDBOARD OR OTHER REFUSE).

A smaller recession in the late 1930s kept the Great Depression from ending, though countries obviously recovered on different schedules. Many historians date the end of the Depression in the U.S. to its entry into World War II, as wartime production invigorated the U.S. economy and the war solved the unemployment crisis (obviously in a less-than-ideal way). Still, it was 1954 before the U.S. stock market hit the highs it had reached right before the '29 crash.

Black Monday

LOCATION: *Global* | TIME FRAME: *1987*

WHEN ECONOMISTS ROUTINELY DESCRIBE ANYTHING AS "WORSE THAN 1929," LET'S JUST SAY IT'S NEVER A GOOD SIGN. ESPECIALLY WHEN THE STOCK MARKET'S INVOLVED.

Black Monday—October 19, 1987—holds the unfortunate title of the single biggest one-day stock-market drop in United States history. The crash actually started in the eastern hemisphere, severely hitting markets in Asia and elsewhere (in Australia and New Zealand, it was actually "Black Tuesday") before heading west over the course of the day.

By spreading backward in terms of time zones, the crash managed to freak out traders who started their workday seeing the sell-off that traders slightly farther east had seen when they started their day. So by the time the panic hit the New York Stock Exchange, it had already wreaked havoc throughout Europe—the London Stock Exchange, for example, took a hit of £50 billion. The Dow Jones Industrial Average fell about 22.6 percent, losing a record total of more than five hundred points.

> IN THE UK, THE OPPOSITION LABOUR PARTY USED A PHOTOGENIC YOUNG POLITICIAN FROM SEDGEFIELD AS ITS SPOKESMAN DURING THE CRISIS: AN MP NAMED TONY BLAIR, WHO WENT ON TO BIGGER THINGS.

WHY THE CRASH? Usually, a one-day crash anywhere near that big has an obvious culprit, but the cause of Black Monday is still a subject of debate more than two decades later. People have blamed everything from a U.S. attack on an Iranian oil platform to the inevitable downturn after a peak to a rush of "program trading" in which computers moved stocks too quickly in reaction to market forces.

In reality, the stock market's perceived value was way too high before the crash, as evidenced by the fact that the Dow Jones managed to finish the year *with a gain* despite the crash—it opened the year at 1,897 points and closed at 1,939. (In August, it had hit a high of 2,722 points—a total it wouldn't see again until 1989.)

The good news was that, unlike in 1929, the stock-market crash didn't signify the coming of a major depression. Some countries were hit particularly hard—New Zealand's stock market saw a 60 percent drop from its 1987 peak—and some took a few years to fully recover, but even investors who took major hits on Black Monday eventually recovered most of their stocks' value if they kept their wits and didn't sell.

> ❋
>
> AFTER THE CRASH, A GROUP OF THIRTY-THREE ECONOMISTS—INCLUDING FIVE NOBEL PRIZE WINNERS—ISSUED A JOINT STATEMENT PREDICTING THE "THE NEXT FEW YEARS COULD BE THE MOST TROUBLED SINCE THE 1930S" IF MARKET INEQUALITIES WEREN'T ADDRESSED. GOOD THING THEY WERE WRONG.
>
> ❋

Dot-Com Bubble

LOCATION: *Global* | TIME FRAME: *1995–2001*

HERE WAS A PERIOD EARLY IN THE INTERNET ERA WHEN MERELY KNOWING POWERPOINT AND BASIC HTML COULD ATTRACT INVESTMENT MONEY—NEVER MIND SUCH TRIVIALITIES AS A BUSINESS PLAN OR THE ABILITY TO TURN A PROFIT.

It made sense that investors wanted to get involved with dot-com businesses in the mid-1990s. After all, the Internet had just become readily accessible to the general public, and (rightly) seemed like the technology of the future. Plus, interest rates were really low, making business investment the logical move.

The problem was there were way too many companies trying to establish themselves in a wide-open environment, which guaranteed that a lot of them wouldn't succeed. And with the whole Internet concept still new to them, speculators got into the habit of investing in anything with an *e-* in front of it or a *.com* at the end, which drove up stock prices for no shortage of really bad business ideas.

A big part of dot-com start-up orthodoxy was that companies would lose money in their first few years, as most of the revenue they took in would be spent on building a bigger market share and overtaking competitors. The thinking was that companies would survive by getting the most customers, then finding a way to make a profit from them. So venture capitalists, angel investors, and even stockholders buying in at the IPO were helping start-ups create revenue with the expectation that profit wouldn't come for years. If they were lucky.

WHY THE CRASH? Things got out of control quickly, with even established companies buying start-ups at hugely inflated prices. Normally sane Mattel bought software developer The Learning Company for $3.5 *billion* in 1999 (and sold it for $27.3 million a year later). Yahoo—itself a 1995 start-up—paid $3.57 billion for GeoCities in 1999.

TO GET A SENSE OF HOW MUCH PEOPLE WANTED TO BELIEVE IN THE POWER OF THE DOT-COM, CONSIDER THESE ACTUAL IDEAS:

• PETS.COM WAS SUPPOSED TO REVOLUTIONIZE THE WAY PEOPLE BOUGHT KITTY LITTER AND DOG TREATS. DESPITE ITS CUTESY PUPPET MASCOT AND HEAVILY HYPED SUPER BOWL ADS, IT JUST NEVER GAVE PEOPLE A GOOD REASON TO BUY ONLINE AND WAIT WHEN THEY COULD JUST POP DOWN TO THE PET STORE FOR ABOUT THE SAME PRICE.

• BEENZ AND FLOOZ OPERATED UNDER THE PREMISE THAT THE PUBLIC WANTED TO SPEND MONEY TO BUY ONLINE-ONLY MONEY FOR ONLINE TRANSACTIONS, INSTEAD OF JUST USING ACTUAL MONEY. THE PUBLIC PREFERRED ACTUAL MONEY.

• GO.COM WAS A DISNEY-OWNED WEB PORTAL THAT CONNECTED ALL KINDS OF OTHERWISE UNRELATED DISNEY-OWNED SITES (FROM ESPN TO RADIO DISNEY) THAT YOU COULD JUST AS EASILY FIND THROUGH SEARCH ENGINES.

• KOZMO.COM DELIVERED A WIDE VARIETY OF ITEMS—FROM MILK TO VIDEO RENTALS TO CONDOMS—TO DOWNTOWN OFFICE BUILDINGS IN SEVERAL MAJOR CITIES. THE RIDICULOUSLY LOW PRICES AND NO-TIP POLICY WERE CONVENIENT FOR CUSTOMERS, BUT PRETTY MUCH GUARANTEED THAT THE COMPANY WOULDN'T MAKE ENOUGH MONEY TO COVER ITS COSTS.

Some companies (like Amazon.com and Google) made the long-term model work. A lot more failed spectacularly. Start-ups became notorious for spending money in ways that would embarrass the most drunken of sailors. Overly elaborate offices and out-of-whack salaries became commonplace. Lots of dot-coms also paid employees in readily available stock, which made them look like millionaires on paper but set them up for a fall. In January 2000, the Super Bowl featured ads by seventeen dot-com companies that spent $2 million each for their half-minute plugs. Typical of the era was Boo.com, an online fashion store that blew through $188 million in just six months before going bankrupt. It seemed that investors were happy to give any bunch of twentysomethings with little or no experience millions to play with, in hopes of getting a big hit.

THE CRASH The peak of the dot-com boom came on March 10, 2000, when the tech-heavy NASDAQ index hit 5,048.62—double its 1999 estimated value. The following weekend (apparently by coincidence), billions of dollars in sell orders for a few prominent tech stocks—including Dell and IBM—spooked the market and started a huge selling trend. Over the next year, many dot-coms went out of business, got sold, or simply lost value. On the plus side, the crash did clear out a lot of really ridiculous companies and forced some slackers to develop more important job skills than dominating at foosball.

Housing Market Crash

LOCATION: *United States* | TIME FRAME: *2007–2010*

AFTER THE DOT-COM BUBBLE BURST, SPECULATORS NEEDED A NEW COMMODITY TO TURN INTO FAST CASH. INSTEAD OF WHERE THEY WORKED, THE FOCUS SHIFTED TO WHERE THEY LIVED. CUE THE MARCH TO INEVITABLE CRISIS.

The American housing market was fertile ground for creating another financial bubble in the early 2000s. The Federal Reserve had lowered interest rates significantly, making it cheaper to borrow money. More importantly, the 1980s and 1990s saw massive deregulation of the financial industry.

Lower interest rates sounded good to speculators, who could buy property and swiftly resell it at a profit. This practice of "flipping" kept driving prices up, and by 2006, average home prices in America had more than doubled from where they were just a decade earlier.

Others bought houses for an old-fashioned reason: to live in them. The now-deregulated banks were happy to oblige—they started giving out home

---

1999'S GRAHAM-LEACH-BLILEY ACT REPEALED BANKING REGULATIONS THAT HAD EXISTED SINCE 1933—ONES PUT IN PLACE SPECIFICALLY TO PREVENT ANOTHER GREAT DEPRESSION. OOPS.

---

loans with little or no money down, often to people with poor credit (an unsound decision on both sides). About four of every five loans to buyers with risky credit—subprime mortgages—had adjustable rates, which started low but increased later. Many borrowers would not be able to afford the mortgage payments once rates shot up, but with no immediate end in sight to the surge in housing prices, that seemed like an insignificant detail.

BY MARCH 2008, ONE IN TEN HOMEOWNERS OWED MORE ON THEIR MORTGAGE THAN THE HOME WAS WORTH.

Meanwhile, banks discovered they could make a profit selling mortgages to other institutions, and using them as guarantees on other financial securities. That made mortgages valuable products in the eyes of investment banks, and the number of these mortgage-backed securities roughly tripled between 1996 and 2007.

THE CRASH It was only a matter of time until this house of cards caught up with itself. By 2007, housing supply far exceeded demand and, for the first time, housing prices fell nationwide. Anyone who had been counting on being able to sell or refinance to cover costs and payments was now in a very bad position, leading to more than a million mortgage defaults and foreclosures.

The cascade left seemingly solid lending institutions so shaky that more than twenty collapsed within a year, with others having to be propped up by government loans. The crashing housing market helped feed (and was fed by) the overall recession in the American (and world) economy in the fall of 2008, and it would be years before prices would recover.

Chapter 2

Mass Hysterias

THE MOST MYSTERIOUS OF PANICS, MASS HYSTERIA COMES IN MANY FORMS. All at once, people either begin experiencing the same physical symptoms or become deluded by the same irrational belief. Some mass hysterias, like the London Monster or the Monkey Man of Delhi, probably started with an incident that gave people a real reason to be scared, and then got blown all out of proportion. Others, like the Dancing Plague that hit sixteenth-century France or the laughing epidemic that infected schoolchildren in modern-day Tanzania, were very real and remain very unexplained. Still others, like Spring-Heeled Jack or the Mad Gasser of Mattoon, might be real or might be completely made up. Whatever the cause, they all inspired mass hysteria.

Dancing Plague

LOCATION: *France* | TIME FRAME: *1518*

RANDOM MASS HYSTERIAS DON'T GET MUCH MORE RANDOM THAN 1518'S BIZARRE DANCING PLAGUE, IN WHICH HUNDREDS OF UNSUSPECTING PEOPLE SUDDENLY STARTED SHOWING OFF KILLER DANCE MOVES. *REALLY* KILLER MOVES, AS MOST OF THE DANCERS DIED DURING THEIR UNCONTROLLABLE DANCE FITS—THE ORIGIN OF WHICH IS STILL A BIG MYSTERY NEARLY FIVE HUNDRED YEARS LATER.

The first victim of the dancing fever was a woman known to history only as Frau Troffea, who on an ordinary July day found herself suddenly (and unintentionally) dancing wildly on a street in Strasbourg, France. She kept dancing for a few days, totally unable to stop. She wasn't alone for long, as the number of helpless dancers filling the street swelled to thirty-four within a week and four hundred by the end of the month.

The people of Strasbourg had absolutely no clue what to do about this sudden dance revolution. This being the sixteenth century, when the area was still part of the Holy Roman Empire, the epidemic got blamed

> WHILE EASILY THE MOST FAMOUS, THE 1518 INCIDENT WAS NOT THE FIRST RECORDED CASE OF A DANCING PLAGUE. IN 1374, TOWNS IN PARTS OF MODERN-DAY BELGIUM AND LUXEMBOURG REPORTED SIMILAR INCIDENTS—BUT NOT AS MUCH IS KNOWN ABOUT THEM.

on everything from demonic possession to "hot blood." Some doctors on the scene figured the only way to stop the dancers was to make them keep going until they tired themselves out. To help with that, the city opened a pair of large halls to provide space for all the hoofers, built a massive stage, and even hired musicians to help them find a beat. The crucial flaw in this plan was that, in many cases, tiring out could prove fatal. Heart attacks, strokes, and deaths by exhaustion became very real problems for the afflicted dancers—and many of them wound up literally dancing themselves to death before the phenomenon mysteriously ended.

WHY THE HYSTERIA? So what prompted the people of Strasbourg to kick up their collective heels? Most of the popular theories have huge flaws. One blames chorea, a disorder that causes involuntary movements, but offers no explanation for why so many people developed the symptoms. Another pins it on a kind of bread mold known for causing hallucinations

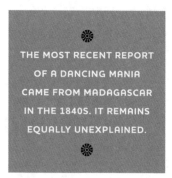

THE MOST RECENT REPORT OF A DANCING MANIA CAME FROM MADAGASCAR IN THE 1840S. IT REMAINS EQUALLY UNEXPLAINED.

and seizures (a phenomenon called "ergotism"). That could explain the number of sufferers, but ergotism also cuts off the blood flow to the limbs, which would make dancing for days physically impossible. One historian claims the Dancing Plague was a psychogenic illness brought on by mass hysteria in a society under stress—and, with famine and disease hitting the area hard, Strasbourg was certainly under stress. Five centuries on, there's a good chance we'll never know what prompted the dangerous dance marathon.

London Monster

A FULL CENTURY BEFORE JACK THE RIPPER MADE LONDON'S DARK ALLEYS DANGEROUS PLACES FOR UNACCOMPANIED WOMEN, THE LONDON MONSTER CONDUCTED HIS OWN REIGN OF TERROR IN THE CITY'S STREETS.

The Monster never killed anyone, but he did attack nearly fifty women between 1788 and 1790. This man would follow a woman, yell a bunch of cruel insults at her, and stab her in the bum with a sharp blade. (Sometimes, he would force a bouquet of fake flowers in her face as a way to get close, then curse at and stab her.) The Monster always escaped before help arrived, and his ability to outsmart the police force added to his legend.

As the attacks continued, the city became a paranoid place. Unsatisfied with the response of London's fledgling police force, lawyer John Julius Angerstein offered an impressive £100 reward for information leading to the Monster's capture. With armed vigilantes already patrolling the streets, the reward led to a series of false accusations. Innocent men grew afraid to approach a woman alone for fear of being labeled the Monster. Some

> ❊
>
> TO PROTECT THEIR POSTERIORS FROM THE MONSTER'S ATTACKS, SOME WEALTHY WOMEN BEGAN WEARING COPPER PETTICOATS. OTHERS RESORTED TO STRATEGICALLY PLACED COOKING POTS UNDER THEIR CLOTHES.
>
> ❊

even created a "No Monster Club" and wore prominent pins to show they were members (and, presumably, not the Monster . . . unless, of course, he had joined as a trick). One thing everyone *did* know about the Monster was that he specifically targeted attractive and usually wealthy women. That led to many unsubstantiated or downright false reports from women who didn't want to be left out, including some self-inflicted buttock stabbings.

THE MONSTER PANIC PROVED A BOON TO LONDON'S PETTY THIEVES. IT BECAME AN EFFECTIVE SCAM TO PICK A MAN'S POCKET, THEN POINT AT HIM AND LOUDLY YELL, "THE MONSTER"—WHICH USUALLY CAUSED ENOUGH COMMOTION TO ENSURE A CLEAN GETAWAY.

THE PINNACLE Things took a turn on June 13, 1790, when previous Monster victim Anne Porter claimed to see her attacker in the park. The accused man, Rhynwick Williams, faced one of history's strangest trials. Authorities wanted him tried as a felon, but English law at the time considered assault a misdemeanor, so he was tried under a 1721 statute making it a felony to tear or deface another's clothing (which was for some reason deemed worse than assault). The courtroom was packed with spectators who openly booed the defense, and the prosecution's top witnesses (Porter and her fiancé) had the conflict-of-interest incentive of getting the reward if Williams was convicted.

The whole thing became such a circus that Williams received a retrial, but despite coworkers vouching for his alibi, he was convicted of misdemeanor charges in three attacks and sentenced to six years in prison. Whether Williams was the Monster or the real one used his conviction as a beard (and historians still debate that), fewer attacks were reported after he was thrown into the pokey.

Spring-Heeled Jack

LOCATION: *Great Britain* | TIME FRAME: *1837–1904*

DEPENDING ON WHOM YOU BELIEVE, SPRING-HEELED JACK WAS A COMMON CRIMINAL, A SUPERNATURAL BEING, OR A FIGMENT OF THE COLLECTIVE IMAGINATION. WHAT EVERYONE AGREED ON WAS THAT HE COULD JUMP REALLY, REALLY HIGH, AND HE WAS NEVER CAUGHT.

The first time anyone heard of Jack was in 1837, when there were three reported sightings. In September, a London businessman claimed to see a man with "devilish features" and glowing eyes leap a ten-foot fence late at night. It sounded like a drunken hallucination, except that in October a mysterious jumping man assaulted a girl named Mary Stevens in a dark alley, gripping her tightly and ripping her clothes with hands she described as feeling cold and "corpse-like." Just one day later, witnesses reportedly saw Jack jump in front of a carriage, causing

THE LEGEND OF SPRING-HEELED JACK HAS INSPIRED SEVERAL STAGE PLAYS, A 1946 MOVIE, A FORTY-EIGHT-PART SERIAL ADVENTURE, AND LOTS OF "PENNY DREADFULS"—SHORT PULPS AIMED AT BRITISH TEENAGERS. HE EVEN MADE AN APPEARANCE IN A JACKIE CHAN CARTOON SHOW AND LENT HIS NAME TO A 1990S SKA BAND.

it to crash, then escape by jumping a wall while laughing maniacally.

WHY THE HYSTERIA? After an article about these sightings appeared in the London papers the following January, reports poured in of similar incidents throughout Britain featuring the devilish figure whose jumping ability earned him his "Spring-Heeled Jack" handle. Dozens of sightings followed, and two February 1838 incidents became huge news stories. Eight days apart, two young girls reported being assaulted by a cloaked figure who spat blue flames at them and grabbed them with claws before fleeing. As Jack's legend grew, his description became even more far-fetched, as witnesses described red eyes, metallic claws, and a helmet (or actual head) featuring satanic horns.

THE MOST RUMORED SUSPECT FOR JACK'S EXPLOITS WAS HENRY BERESFORD. KNOWN AS THE "MAD MARQUIS" (HE *WAS* AN ACTUAL NOBLEMAN), HE HAD A REPUTATION FOR DRINKING AND LEWD BEHAVIOR, AND WAS BASED IN LONDON AT THE TIME. NO LINK TO JACK (OR ANY JUMPING PROWESS) WAS EVER PROVEN, AND JACK SIGHTINGS CONTINUED LONG AFTER THE 1859 DEATH OF THE MARQUIS.

In his heyday, Jack was accused in a number of incidents, from causing carriage crashes to throwing a prostitute into a sewer. His last famous appearance came in 1877, when he reportedly slapped a soldier with his cold hands and survived getting shot before escaping. Britons still claimed to see him from time to time, with the last reported sighting in 1904. The wide range of reports added to Jack's legend, but also made him notoriously hard to pin down. Maybe he was one man, or a series of copycats. Maybe he was real and exaggerated, or just an urban legend that took on a life of its own. Nobody really knows Jack.

The War of the Worlds Broadcast

Location: *United States* | Time Frame: *1938*

A NUMBER OF MOVIES AND PLAYS HAVE TRIED TO SCARE PEOPLE WITH THE IDEA OF ALIENS DESTROYING THE PLANET, BUT NOBODY HAS EVER USED ALIENS TO SCARE THE BEJESUS OUT OF THE PUBLIC MORE SUCCESSFULLY THAN ORSON WELLES.

When the twenty-two-year-old Welles and his Mercury Theatre on the Air performed a version of the H. G. Wells (no relation) classic *The War of the Worlds* on October 30, 1938, his goal was to create a memorable Halloween show and stage the biggest fictional destruction of New York since *King Kong* five years earlier.

Published in 1898, the Wells novel was a revolutionary masterpiece—the book that introduced to popular fiction the idea of an invasion from outer space. The story involves aliens coming to Earth in giant tripod machines that make short work of the human race—definite potential for a good scare, especially in the hands of the right performer.

Enter Welles, a prodigy who made his stage debut as a teenager while traveling in Ireland. The New Deal–funded Federal Theatre had hired him to direct plays in New York until he clashed with the program over its "budget cuts" for *The Cradle Will Rock*—Welles (and others) saw "budget cuts" as a nice way of saying "the play was way too political." In response, Welles put together his own troupe and named it the Mercury Theatre.

While performing around New York, the group also started moonlighting on the radio and eventually got a primo gig with CBS to perform weekly radio plays based on classic literature. By Halloween 1938, the show had been on the air for seventeen weeks—presumably long enough for people to know about it. Also, like all previous episodes, *The War of the Worlds* broadcast was advertised in all the usual places and listed in the programming schedule. Too many people just missed all those clues.

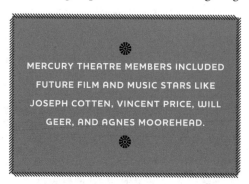

MERCURY THEATRE MEMBERS INCLUDED FUTURE FILM AND MUSIC STARS LIKE JOSEPH COTTEN, VINCENT PRICE, WILL GEER, AND AGNES MOOREHEAD.

WHY THE HYSTERIA? To be fair, it wasn't just people who believed "gullible" wasn't in the dictionary; Welles made a few staging choices that made *The War of the Worlds* sound like an actual (though one-sided) war of the worlds. He moved the setting of the story from Victorian England to modern-day America. He adapted its first-person, journalistic style by telling much of the tale via radio "news bulletins" covering the invasion in real time. And he made it sound as much like real catastrophe coverage as possible by having the news bulletins constantly interrupting a simulated "program of dance music." Needless to say, soon nobody was paying much attention to the music.

Early "bulletins" included an astronomer observing strange explosions on Mars, an extraterrestrial cylinder landing near Grover's Mill, New Jersey, and a tripod machine emerging from the crash site. Within an hour, the alien tripod was reported to have defeated seven thousand armed men, joined up with other invaders to attack New York City, and released a deadly black smoke that left thousands of people "falling like flies."

Without the effects budget of *Independence Day*, Welles and his crew had to rely on some brilliant theater-of-the-mind touches, including a spot-on speech by the secretary of the interior (Welles trusted that the public didn't pay enough attention to know who the real one was), realistic audio of the military firing in vain at the invaders, people screaming in fear, and—most convincingly—a short-lived "correspondent" describing the cloud of smoke as it approaches him before coughing and falling silent. Probably the best radio death ever.

THE STORY OF THE PANIC BECAME SO WELL KNOWN THAT ADOLF HITLER LATER CITED IT IN HIS OFFICIAL PROPAGANDA AS PROOF OF AMERICANS' GULLIBILITY.

THE PINNACLE For listeners who stayed tuned in for the entire show, this was just great radio. The problem? Those darned channel surfers, who had to spoil the fun for everybody. Those who failed to read the radio listings or hear any of the program's *three* identification breaks tuned in and freaked out in what the next day's *New York Times* described as "a wave of mass hysteria."

The police in East Orange, New Jersey, reportedly received two hundred calls from people asking how they could flee the gas cloud. There were reports of families running from their homes, a bus dispatcher altering a route to avoid the aliens, and churches holding emergency "end of the world" services. Even geniuses fell for it—two Princeton geologists raced to the "crash site" in hopes of examining the meteor. Some people even insisted they actually *saw* the gas cloud or the invading spacecraft.

THE AFTERMATH A few weeks later, roughly 12 million people told a pollster that they had heard the broadcast. There's no way that could be true—it would be ridiculously high compared to earlier episodes, and the show didn't become legendary until after *The War of the Worlds* program aired. As for Welles, he was all for the publicity, which made him a national celebrity and put him on the fast track to a film career as an actor and director.

⁜

AFTER *THE WAR OF THE WORLDS*, RATINGS FOR THE MERCURY THEATRE PROGRAM SKYROCKETED. THE CAMPBELL'S SOUP COMPANY SOON JOINED AS A SPONSOR, WITH THE SHOW RENAMED *THE CAMPBELL PLAYHOUSE.*

Mad Gasser of Mattoon

LOCATION: *United States* | TIME FRAME: *1944*

DURING WORLD WAR II, A SMALL TOWN IN WESTERN ILLINOIS BECAME THE SCENE OF A STILL-UNSOLVED CASE OF MASS HYSTERIA. AND THIS ONE, IN FACT, WAS A GAS.

The first reports of a Mad Gasser lurking in the town of Mattoon came on August 31, 1944. A man awoke in the middle of the night to an unrecognizable, strong odor from a presumed gas leak that made him throw up and left his wife temporarily paralyzed in bed. Later that night, a neighbor reported being unable to leave her bed when she woke up to her daughter coughing in the middle of the night.

So there's the gas; now for the gasser. On September 1, Mrs. Bert Kearney reported smelling a strong odor during the night. She claimed the stench became progressively stronger and caused her to lose feeling in her legs. Her sister noticed the same smell, and the women called the police. When Mrs. Kearney's husband

THE MYSTERIOUS GASSER WAS GIVEN A NUMBER OF NICKNAMES, INCLUDING THE MAD ANESTHETIST, THE PHANTOM ANESTHETIST, AND THE ANESTHETIC PROWLER.

came home about ninety minutes after his wife first smelled the gas, he reportedly saw a mysterious man outside their window who ran away when he approached. He said the man wore all black, with a tight-fitting cap, and held some kind of device in his hand. That description, once published in the local paper, became known as the uniform of the Mad Gasser.

THE PINNACLE Between August 31 and September 13, Mattoon police received more than a dozen reports of the mysterious gas.

A DECADE BEFORE THE MATTOON INCIDENTS, AN ODDLY SIMILAR SERIES OF UNSOLVED ATTACKS WAS REPORTED NEAR ROANOKE, VIRGINIA. VICTIMS REPORTED STRANGE, SWEET FUMES AND CONVULSING, VOMITING, OR TEMPORARY PARALYSIS. THE TWELVE ATTACKS OCCURRED BETWEEN DECEMBER 1933 AND FEBRUARY 1934.

Some also reported seeing the Mad Gasser, while others reported evidence of his presence. One woman found a white handkerchief on her porch that caused a burning sensation in her throat after she smelled it.

By September 12, Mattoon police had gotten so many false alarms that they stopped giving priority to Mad Gasser reports, and just two weeks after they started, the Mad Gasser attacks stopped abruptly after September 13. It's possible that there was an actual maniac responsible for some of the gas attacks—though it's unclear how many attacks were real and how many were hysteria-induced. It's also possible, as the Mattoon chief of police speculated at the time, that toxic waste from the nearby Atlas-Imperial diesel plant played a role. The company had carbon tetrachloride—a chemical with a sweet, strong smell that could cause the alleged symptoms—on-site at the time, but denied there was enough to sicken people (and noted no employees got sick).

Tanganyika Laughter Epidemic

LOCATION: *Tanzania/Tanganyika* | TIME FRAME: *1962*

IF THE CLICHÉ ABOUT LAUGHTER BEING THE BEST MEDICINE IS TRUE, THE VILLAGE OF KASHASHA GOT DANGEROUSLY HEALTHY IN 1962.

The whole thing started in an all-girls school in a small village near Lake Victoria in what was then Tanganyika. On January 30, for no clear reason, three young girls broke into sudden fits of laughter during the middle of the school day and weren't able to stop.

Their laughter proved literally uncontrollable, as teachers were unable to stop the fits or even restrain the girls. The laughter also proved highly, highly contagious.

> QUICK GEOGRAPHY LESSON:
> TANGANYIKA LATER MERGED WITH
> ZANZIBAR TO FORM MODERN TANZANIA.

It was only a matter of days before most of the girls' classmates—reportedly 95 of the school's 159 students—were laughing hysterically, many to the point of crying. The symptoms went from funny to scary in a hurry, with laughing fits lasting anywhere from a few intense minutes to hours on end, with girls experiencing multiple fits at random for as long as two weeks. The fits also led to all kinds of other side effects, including gas, rashes, and fainting.

WHY THE HYSTERIA? With this being the first reported incident of its kind, teachers had no blueprint for what to do. Things got

❉

ODDLY, THE THREE TEACHERS AT THE SCHOOL MANAGED TO AVOID CATCHING THE LAUGHTER FITS, SUGGESTING AGE MIGHT HAVE BEEN A FACTOR.

❉

so bad that, on March 18, the school sent all of its students home and closed for three days. That hardly worked, as most of the students who hadn't yet caught the laughing fits did so within days of the reopening, forcing the school to shut down again. The laughing fits weren't confined to the building, either. Several schoolgirls from the nearby village of Nshamba brought their symptoms home, and that village saw 217 cases of laughing fits.

In fact, a number of villages around Lake Victoria—mostly in Tanganyika but also in Uganda—suffered laughing attacks. Before the epidemic ended, it had spread to at least fourteen schools and infected at least a thousand people, most of them school-age children. Quarantining "infected" villages and schools proved the only effective way to stop the laughter from spreading, though it did nothing to stop those already stricken. By June 1964, the laughter stopped the same way it started—suddenly and for no obvious reason.

Luckily, nobody died or suffered long-term illness as a result of the fits. Oddly, despite it happening in modern times and scientists conducting serious research on the ground, nobody has any idea what caused the laughter. Attempts to locate a virus, gas leak, or other pathogen in the victims turned up nothing. In short, the epidemic left experts baffled as to what was so funny.

Villejuif Leaflet

WHILE MOST CHAIN LETTERS PROMISE BAD LUCK IF YOU DON'T PASS THEM ON TO TEN FRIENDS, THE MISSIVE KNOWN AS THE "VILLEJUIF LEAFLET" HAD AN EQUALLY DUBIOUS BUT MORE PANIC-INDUCING MESSAGE.

The one-page, typewritten leaflet was first reported in France sometime in February 1976, and to this day, it's unclear where it came from. It contained a list of various food additives, and broke them down into three lists according to whether they were harmless, possibly harmless, or dangerous carcinogens that would infect you and everybody you knew with cancer. The leaflet also singled out specific brands (including big names like Schweppes and Coca-Cola) and specific chemicals (most famously E330, which is merely citric acid and present in most fruits and veggies) as deadly causes of cancer.

The claims were all complete rubbish, but that didn't stop the leaflet from spreading. Well-meaning recipients naturally wanted to warn their

CITRIC ACID IS CRUCIAL TO THE BODY'S CITRIC-ACID CYCLE, A PROCESS KNOWN AS THE "KREBS CYCLE." ONE THEORY FOR THE LEAFLET'S EXISTENCE BLAMES A TRANSLATION ERROR, AS *KREBS* IS GERMAN FOR "CANCER."

friends and families, and the pamphlet got passed along like a hot potato. The leaflet also managed to list some actual carcinogens as harmless, adding an extra layer of inaccuracy.

WHY THE HYSTERIA? The memo was nicknamed the "Villejuif Leaflet" because, after it had already circulated for a few years, the version going around listed its source as "the Hospital at Villejuif" (an area in the Paris suburbs). That no hospital went by the name didn't end the panic. Nor did

> IN ONE DENUNCIATION OF THE LEAFLET, THE VILLEJUIF HOSPITAL'S DIRECTOR, MAURICE TUBIANA, SAID, "EVERY SCIENTIST WHO HAS READ IT HAS BURST OUT LAUGHING AT ITS LOAD OF INANITIES."

the fact that the hospital in Villejuif that was obviously being referred to—the Gustave-Roussy Institute, a facility famous for its expertise in the treatment of cancer—consistently pointed out that it had nothing to do with the leaflet and that the leaflet's claims were pure poppycock. Companies named in the leaflet obviously did their best to debunk the claims as well, but the fear persisted. (At one point, a survey found that one in five French households reported boycotting the brands the leaflet deemed cancer-causing, and nearly 70 percent considered doing so).

Even some professionals were fooled, with several newspapers and one book about cancer (by a doctor, no less) reprinting the leaflet's false claims as if they were true. After a decade of misleading the public, the letter's popularity petered out by around 1986, by which point it had reached about seven million people and been passed around several countries in Europe, Africa, and the Middle East.

Fan Death

LOCATION: *South Korea* | TIME FRAME: *1970s–present*

NEVER MIND THAT IT'S PHYSICALLY IMPOSSIBLE, OR THAT IT'S BEEN DEBUNKED OVER AND OVER AND OVER. THERE'S STILL A SEGMENT OF THE KOREAN POPU-LATION THAT REALLY THINKS ELECTRIC FANS DOUBLE AS SERIAL KILLERS.

The so-called fan death supposedly happens when you fall asleep in a closed room with an electric fan running, and then fail to wake up. South Koreans have been reporting these deaths for years, almost always during the summer months. A 1997 article in *The Korean Herald* blamed ten deaths during that summer's heat wave on "the effects of electric fans" (as opposed to, you know, the heat wave). Nearly every summer heat wave in Korea brings new news reports of death by fan. There was even a 1973 fan death case where the deceased was also found with an unexplained and rather suspicious "jar of chemicals" in the room—but the public blamed his two fans and closed door instead.

> DESPITE THE SAME EXACT FANS BEING USED IN MANY COUNTRIES, NO FAN DEATH CASES HAVE EVER BEEN REPORTED OUTSIDE KOREA.

WHY THE HYSTERIA? As you've probably guessed, fan death is the worst kind of pseudoscience. While many Koreans believe in this breezy urban legend, they have wildly different theories for why fans supposedly turn deadly. Some believe the fans cause hypothermia by blowing cold air on a sleeping body and dangerously decreasing body temperature. Never mind that fans aren't able to lower body temperature, which is the reason they aren't effective antidotes to heatstroke. Nor do fans actually chill the air; they just circulate it. Others claim the "victims" die of asphyxiation as their breathing replaces the oxygen in the room with carbon dioxide (which is possible in very rare cases in an unventilated room, but has nothing to do with whether a fan is running). Some Koreans blame fans for suffocation, or—in perhaps the wackiest version—claim fan blades somehow chop up microscopic oxygen molecules.

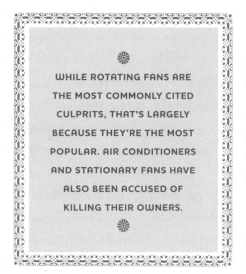

WHILE ROTATING FANS ARE THE MOST COMMONLY CITED CULPRITS, THAT'S LARGELY BECAUSE THEY'RE THE MOST POPULAR. AIR CONDITIONERS AND STATIONARY FANS HAVE ALSO BEEN ACCUSED OF KILLING THEIR OWNERS.

In 2006, South Korea's Consumer Protection Board—an actual government body that should know better—published a safety alert that listed fan death among the country's biggest summer hazards. The alert blamed fan death on asphyxiation, and advised people to keep their doors open at night. Other official sources take the same line, with major newspapers and even medical professionals in Korea publicly supporting this easily discredited theory, even as several studies conducted in other countries (including the United States) demonstrated that fans are innocent of all charges. Still, all electric fans sold in Korea come with a "timer knob" to shut them off after a certain number of rotations— before they can allegedly strike.

Monkey Man of Delhi

Location: *India* | Time Frame: *2001*

IN 2001, A MYSTERIOUS CREATURE TERRORIZED THE INDIAN CITY OF DELHI. IT'S UNCLEAR WHO OR WHAT THE MONKEY MAN OF DELHI ACTUALLY WAS, BUT ONE THING IS CERTAIN—HE DID A LOT MORE THAN THROW POOP.

During a particularly hot season in the crowded capital, many of Delhi's residents took to sleeping on rooftops to cool down. That made them easy prey for the mysterious nocturnal attacker, with the first attack reported April 5. By May 13, fifteen people had reported being scratched, bitten, or otherwise assaulted by what they described as a four-foot, dark-haired, human-animal hybrid. During the peak of the hysteria, the Monkey Man attacked at least a hundred people, and some attacks were quite serious. A pregnant woman fell down a flight of stairs in fear after neighbors claimed to see the simian stalker, and at least one man fell off a roof to his death while trying to escape the Monkey Man's claws.

EVEN BOLLYWOOD GOT IN ON THE MANIA. THE 2006 FILM *DELHI-9* INCLUDES A SUBPLOT WHERE THE MAIN CHARACTER DONS A MONKEY MASK AND LEAPS FROM ROOFTOP TO ROOFTOP AS A WAY OF STEALTHILY TRACKING A ROMANTIC RIVAL.

WHY THE HYSTERIA? Because eyewitness accounts varied wildly—and nobody ever captured a photo or video of the attacker—the Monkey Man took on otherworldly qualities, adding to the panic. Descriptions ranged from the plausible (a very large macaque monkey) to the weird (a man in costume with coil springs on his feet) to the supernatural (the embodiment of the monkey deity Hanuman). Eyewitnesses variously described him as wearing a helmet, using metal claws, and having glowing red eyes. Some claimed he was a metal robot with buttons on his chest, or one of several Monkey Men working together, or even a Pakistani spy. One consistent theme was that the furry marauder could leap from rooftop to rooftop easily, and sprint remarkably quickly during his getaways.

> ✻
>
> THE MONKEY MAN HYSTERIA DID HAVE ONE POSITIVE SIDE EFFECT: DELHI POLICE REPORTED A HUGE DROP IN THE CITY'S CRIME RATE DURING THE PEAK OF THE FEAR, AS EXTRA-VIGILANT CITIZENS (OFTEN ARMED ONES) SCARED AWAY ANY NUMBER OF WOULD-BE THIEVES AND NE'ER-DO-WELLS.
>
> ✻

Police worked overtime to catch the Monkey Man, with extra patrols and shoot-to-kill orders. They passed out multiple (and contradictory) sketch-artist renditions of the attacker, and brought in zoo officials to try identifying potential primate pests. Scared citizens even took the law into their own hands, and mobs assaulted at least two hirsute men who too closely resembled descriptions of the Monkey Man. The attacks ultimately died down by the end of the summer, and despite a few more sightings, the culprit—and a plausible explanation—was never identified.

Soap Opera Disease

LOCATION: *Portugal* | TIME FRAME: *2006*

WE ALL LIKE IT WHEN OUR FAVORITE TELEVISION SHOW FEATURES CHARAC-
TERS WE CAN RELATE TO, BUT THERE ARE LIMITS. GETTING SICK BECAUSE
OF SOMETHING THAT HAPPENS ON THE SMALL SCREEN IS PROBABLY A GOOD PLACE TO
DRAW THAT LINE.

The show that inspired the sickness in question is the Portuguese soap opera *Morangos com Açúcar* (which translates as either "Strawberries with Sugar" or "Sweet Strawberries"). Since its 2003 debut, Portuguese teens and tweens have tuned in to the daily soap in huge numbers, making it one of the country's most successful youth-oriented shows. *Morangos* features everything you'd expect from a teen soap—a cast of mostly models with a fairly high turn-over, over-the-top dialogue, and any number of seemingly out-of-nowhere plot devices.

> "CELEBRITIES" WHO HAVE APPEARED ON *MORANGOS* INCLUDE BRITISH SOUL BAND SIMPLY RED, REGGAE RAPPER SEAN KINGSTON, AND FORMER SPICE GIRL MELANIE C.

One of *Morangos*'s big plot twists came during a single May 2006 episode in which a potentially killer virus infects the school most of the characters attend. Now here's the weird part. Within days of the airing of that episode, lots of real kids claimed to have the exact same symptoms the *Morangos* characters suffered from this imaginary virus. Reuters news service reported at the time that more than three hundred students at fourteen different schools—spread throughout Portugal—were complaining about rashes, dizziness, or trouble breathing.

WHY THE HYSTERIA? Of course, what became known as the "Strawberries with Sugar Virus" wasn't a real disease (that it attacked only teenagers who watched one show ranked among the more obvious signs). "What we concretely have is a few children with allergies and apparently a phenomenon of many other children imitating," the director of Portugal's National Institute for Medical Emergencies reported at the time, and the institute dubbed the whole incident a case of

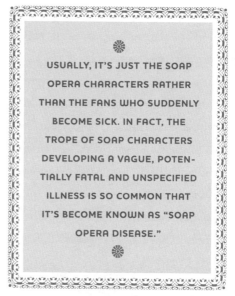

USUALLY, IT'S JUST THE SOAP OPERA CHARACTERS RATHER THAN THE FANS WHO SUDDENLY BECOME SICK. IN FACT, THE TROPE OF SOAP CHARACTERS DEVELOPING A VAGUE, POTENTIALLY FATAL AND UNSPECIFIED ILLNESS IS SO COMMON THAT IT'S BECOME KNOWN AS "SOAP OPERA DISEASE."

"mass hysteria." Some students seemed to overreact to real but minor breathing problems and rashes, while for others, the whole thing was purely psychosomatic. The outbreak also might have had something to do with nervousness about (or an attempt to avoid) the end-of-year exams students throughout Portugal were taking the same week the hysteria broke out.

Shark Attacks

LOCATION: *United States* | TIME FRAME: *1916, 1970s, 2000s*

SHARKS ONLY KILL ABOUT FIVE PEOPLE A YEAR—SLIGHTLY FEWER THAN DIE FROM GETTING CRUSHED BY VENDING MACHINES—BUT THERE'S JUST SOMETHING ABOUT THE SIZE OF THOSE TEETH THAT MAKES PEOPLE DOUBT THAT IT'S SAFE TO GO BACK IN THE WATER.

The predatory fish have a long history of terrifying people. Occasional shark attacks have troubled sailors and fishermen for ages, but the first shark attacks to prompt widespread panic in the American public happened off the Jersey shore in 1916. Five people were attacked, four fatally, at three far-flung spots along the New Jersey coast in the span of just eleven days. The "Jersey man-eater" attacks made national news, prompted a large-scale shark hunt, and became the basis for lots of sensationalist stories that helped the public view sharks as

ONE OF THE MOST HORRIFIC SHARK ATTACKS IN HISTORY HAPPENED NEAR GUAM DURING WORLD WAR II. WHEN THE *USS INDIANAPOLIS* WAS HIT BY JAPANESE TORPEDOES, NEARLY NINE HUNDRED SAILORS SURVIVED THE EXPLOSION AND SINKING BUT FOUND THEMSELVES STRANDED IN SHARK-INFESTED WATER, WITH THEIR COLLEAGUES' BLOOD DRAWING THE FISH. WHILE NOT ALL OF THE SUBSEQUENT DEATHS COULD BE DIRECTLY ATTRIBUTED TO THE SHARKS, ONLY ABOUT THREE HUNDRED SAILORS WERE PULLED FROM THE WATER ALIVE.

far more dangerous than they actually are. That idea was reinforced by a few World War II incidents in which crews of sinking ships jumped overboard, and the blood of dead men drew sharks to attack the survivors.

DA DUM . . . DA DUM . . . DA-DUM-DA-DUM-DA-DUM Masses of people became scared again in the mid-1970s by shark attacks that weren't even real. Peter Benchley's 1974 pulp novel *Jaws*, about a great white ruining many a vacation at a seaside resort, was a major bestseller. The following summer, Steven Spielberg's movie adaptation (widely considered the first true summer blockbuster and the highest-grossing movie ever at the time) got blamed for beach resorts struggling all summer as tourists were scared of what might be lurking near the shore.

❋

BENCHLEY REPUDIATED THE FEAR HIS WORK INSPIRED, SAYING IN 2000, "CONSIDERING THE KNOWLEDGE ACCUMULATED ABOUT SHARKS IN THE LAST 25 YEARS, I COULDN'T POSSIBLY WRITE *JAWS* TODAY." HE BECAME A DEDICATED OCEANIC CONSERVATIONIST, SPEAKING OUT AGAINST THE DESTRUCTION OF SHARKS— EITHER FOR SPORT OR FOR COMMERCE—AND WRITING SEVERAL NONFICTION BOOKS IN DEFENSE OF THE MISUNDERSTOOD FISH.

❋

"SUMMER OF THE SHARK" Shark attacks again actively captured the American public's imagination in the summer of 2000, when an unusually high number of attacks against humans led to another round of panic. A total of seventy-nine shark attacks were reported that year worldwide—nearly half of them in Florida. Only eleven were fatal, and even that made it well above an average year. The following summer, despite a significant *drop* in attacks, a few high-profile incidents—like a bull shark biting off a child's arm in July 2001—drove relentless media coverage of what became known as "Summer of the Shark."

Of course, sharks don't actually prey on humans. Most bites are merely exploratory, as the animals mistake the person for something else and then move on—though such bites can still cause serious injury. Very few of the attacks recorded throughout history have involved sharks actually eating people and—of more than 360 shark species—only the great white, tiger shark, bull shark, and whitetip have been known to attack humans unless directly provoked. The reality is sharks are the ones who should be afraid—while they kill about five people each year, humans kill more than a million sharks (many of them endangered species) annually.

THE UNITED STATES LEADS THE WORLD IN REPORTED SHARK ATTACKS, FOLLOWED BY AUSTRALIA AND SOUTH AFRICA. NEW SMYRNA BEACH ON FLORIDA'S EAST COAST IS THE WORLD'S TOP SHARK-ATTACK HOT SPOT.

Chapter 3

Moral Panics

ONE PERSON'S GOOD TIME IS ANOTHER'S VICE, AND HIS-
TORY HAS THOUSANDS OF EXAMPLES OF CULTURE CLASHES
THAT HAVE CAUSED EXTREME OVERREACTIONS. Some moral
panics involve persecution and witch hunts (for actual
witches or for citizens deemed insufficiently "capitalistic").
Some involve censorship to keep readers from experiencing
sexual thrills or children from learning naughty language.
Some arise from genuine if unfounded fears, whether of
children joining orgies, dice games turning kids into killers,
or the wrong music inspiring suicidal tendencies. Blame
religion, blame society, blame peer pressure and mass hysteria. But some busybody is always going to be just a little
too worried about what the neighbors are up to.

Witch Hunts

LOCATION: *Europe* | TIME FRAME: *1300s–1700s*

FEARS OF WITCHCRAFT GO BACK TO AROUND THE YEAR 1000, WHEN RELIGIOUS FOLKS STARTED WORRYING THAT SATAN AND HIS FOLLOWERS WERE NOT JUST EVIL FORCES BUT ACTUAL PEOPLE HANGING OUT AMONG THEM.

Credit for the wave of European witch trials often goes to Pope John XXII, whose own fears about sorcery led him to authorize the notorious Inquisition to add witchcraft to the list of prosecutable heresies in 1320. And thanks to a passage in the Book of Exodus ("Thou shalt not suffer a witch to live"), witch hunters were basically given a license to kill.

> THE ROMAN CATHOLIC CHURCH IN THE MIDDLE AGES WASN'T AGAINST MAGIC PER SE. IT DREW DISTINCTIONS BETWEEN THE "POSITIVE" MAGIC OF FOLK PRACTITIONERS AND THE "DARK" MAGIC OF WITCHCRAFT.

Kill they did, with a few waves of witch fears passing through various European countries over the following centuries. The fourteenth-century hysteria about witches peaked around the time the Black Plague hit Europe, when previously unimaginable numbers of the population were dying and doctors didn't yet understand the cause of the illness. As clergy members died at roughly the same rate as other people, the idea that black magic was behind the plague led to the murder of hundreds of suspected witches (and of innocent non-Christians in general). Anything from an unusual birthmark to a public disagreement with the Church to an affinity for black cats could get an innocent person labeled a witch.

WHY THE PANIC? Witch hunts became more formal with the advent of witch trials. The first major one on record took place in Germany in the 1500s, and Germany was the worst offender overall—the southwest part of the country alone saw more than three thousand people convicted and executed between 1561 and 1670. Trials varied widely, with some employing torture in order to extract confessions and others becoming post-Reformation proxy wars between Catholics and Protestants slinging charges at each other. Witch trials and executions—usually by burning or hanging—were recorded in nearly every European country, with France, Switzerland, and Poland racking up the bloodiest totals outside Germany.

THE IDEA OF WITCHCRAFT IS TRULY OLD-SCHOOL. THE CODE OF HAMMURABI—FROM BABYLON, IN THE 1700S BCE—HAD PROVISIONS FOR WHAT TO DO IF A MAN PUT A SPELL ON ANOTHER WITHOUT CAUSE.

Eventually, more enlightened heads prevailed. England's last witchcraft execution came in 1716, Germany's in 1738, and Poland's in 1793—the last "official" witch trial in Europe. Nobody's sure exactly how many women—and they were mostly women—died during the waves of European witch hunts. About twelve thousand executions were officially recorded, but historians estimate the total number could be four to ten times that many.

Salem Witch Trials

LOCATION: *United States* | TIME FRAME: *1692–1693*

NEVER DOUBT THE POWER OF CHILDREN'S IMAGINATIONS. ALL IT TOOK TO LAUNCH THE SALEM WITCH TRIALS WERE A FEW YOUNG GIRLS SPINNING WILD STORIES AND ACCUSING SPECIFIC TOWNSPEOPLE OF CASTING SPELLS. BY THE TIME THE PANIC DIED DOWN, TWENTY PEOPLE HAD BEEN EXECUTED AND MORE THAN A HUNDRED IMPRISONED.

The whole thing started with two cousins, Betty Parris and Abigail Williams, who in February 1692 fell ill with strange symptoms. It's still unclear if their illness was real, psychosomatic, or just made up to get attention. What the people at the time did know was that the illness seemed a lot like the symptoms described in Cotton Mather's recent book on witchcraft, and a doctor who examined the girls blamed supernatural forces for their ailment. Considering that superstitions about witchcraft claimed witches targeted kids, and that more girls soon developed the same symptoms,

⊰※⊱

WHILE SALEM GETS MOST OF THE PUBLICITY, THE TRIALS LUMPED TOGETHER AS THE SALEM WITCH TRIALS TOOK PLACE IN A NUMBER OF TOWNS IN THE AREA, INCLUDING BOSTON, IPSWICH, CHARLESTOWN, AND ANDOVER.

it soon seemed plausible to the Puritanical town that the Salem area was absolutely crawling with witchcraft.

Accusations followed quickly, starting with the interrogation and imprisonment of three women named by the girls. One of them, a slave named Tituba, made things worse by confessing under pressure to working on behalf of the devil and saying she and other accused women

SALEM STILL TRADES ON ITS REPUTATION. IT IS HOME TO THE SALEM WITCH MUSEUM, SALEM WITCH VILLAGE, AND THE WITCHES' LEAGUE FOR PUBLIC AWARENESS. EVERY OCTOBER, THE TOWN HOSTS NIGHTLY TOURS OF WITCH-TRIAL SITES AND A BIG HALLOWEEN BALL.

had flown through the air on sticks. Her "confession" sparked a hunt for more witches, and dozens of arrests followed. And the girls' hysterical, "possessed" testimony in court made the accused witches seem more immediately dangerous.

WHY THE PANIC? Starting with barmaid Bridget Bishop on June 10, nineteen people were hanged. Another four died in prison, and eighty-year-old Giles Corey was crushed to death with stones when he refused to enter a plea in what he (rightly) deemed a sham trial. Anyone who spoke out against the witch hunt became a potential target. The last eight executions were carried out in September, by which point Salem's leaders were beginning to doubt the widespread charges against increasingly respectable townspeople. In May 1693, the governor of Massachusetts stepped in and brought the panic to a close, releasing more than a hundred alleged witches from prison. The people of Salem seemed to have learned their lesson, and nobody in America was arrested for witchcraft from that point forward.

McCarthyism

LOCATION: *United States* | TIME FRAME: *1940s–1950s*

NOT ALL WITCH HUNTS INVOLVE ACCUSATIONS OF BLACK MAGIC AND WORKING IN LEAGUE WITH THE DEVIL. THOUGH ANYONE CAUGHT UP IN FAR-RIGHT-WING SENATOR JOE MCCARTHY'S PARANOID VERSION MIGHT HAVE THOUGHT THOSE ACCUSATIONS DIDN'T SEEM SO BAD BY COMPARISON.

The Republican senator from Wisconsin had a fairly quiet career at the national level until a speech in West Virginia on February 9, 1950, when he held up a piece of paper he claimed was a list of "known Communists" working in the State Department. Never mind that McCarthy pulled the list directly from his own posterior or that the paper he held in his hand didn't actually contain the names. In his own runs for office, he'd also shown a disturbing tendency to accuse his opponents of being in league with Communists. At a time when Cold War paranoia was rampant, accusations of supporting Communists (and, by extension, the Soviet Union) ruined careers and reputations, and McCarthy enjoyed doing so. Within a few weeks, the term "McCarthyism" had become the brand name for all anti-Communist witch hunts.

McCarthy took the term as a compliment, even using it as a title when he published an anti-Communist manifesto in 1952, and few doubted the sincerity of his obsession. The Republican establishment wasn't quite sure what to do with him and, at the start of his second term in 1953, made him chairman of the Senate Committee on Government Operations. In theory, that post should have kept McCarthy from getting out of control. Instead, he turned a subcommittee previously tasked with investigating war crimes and defense contracts into the Senate Permanent Committee on Investigations and used it to launch investigations into allegations he himself had made against supposed Communists.

WHY THE PANIC? McCarthy first targeted Voice of America, the State Department's international radio and TV wing, claiming it was secretly broadcasting subversive messages. McCarthy couldn't prove his charges, but the televised hearings and his aggressive questioning made him an even bigger star than he already was. (He drove at least one stressed-out VOA employee to suicide.) McCarthy then scored a victory when his investigations got the State Department to remove books he deemed subversive from its overseas libraries. (A move President Dwight Eisenhower criticized, urging the public not to join the "book burners.")

⋇

BECAUSE OF THEIR SIMILAR OBSESSIONS WITH COMMUNISTS, THE HOUSE UN-AMERICAN ACTIVITIES COMMITTEE OFTEN GETS LUMPED IN WITH MCCARTHY, EVEN THOUGH IT PREDATED AND DIDN'T INVOLVE HIM. HUAC WAS STARTED IN 1938, INVESTIGATING GERMAN-AMERICAN INVOLVEMENT IN WARTIME WHITE-SUPREMACIST GROUPS. BY 1947, HOWEVER, IT WAS BEST KNOWN FOR ITS INVESTIGATIONS INTO ALLEGED COMMUNIST ACTIVITY IN HOLLYWOOD— HEARINGS THAT INITIATED THE INFAMOUS HOLLYWOOD BLACKLIST. HUAC MANAGED TO USE FALSE CHARGES TO DESTROY MANY, MANY CAREERS BEFORE IT CLOSED SHOP IN 1975.

McCarthy's next investigation, into the promotion of supposed Communists in the army, ultimately proved to be his undoing. With support from the president, army officials turned the tables and questioned McCarthy in front of his own committee, during thirty-six days of hearings on live television. Initially about McCarthy's demands for special treatment of his army allies, the hearings turned into a referendum on McCarthy's tactics overall. The senator, whose popularity with the public peaked in early 1954, saw his approval rating fall from 50 percent to 34 percent in no time.

> MCCARTHY'S FALSE ALLEGATIONS AGAINST THE STATE DEPARTMENT CAUSED PRESIDENT HARRY TRUMAN TO CALL THE WISCONSIN SENATOR "THE BEST ASSET THE KREMLIN HAS."

When McCarthy refused to supply the committee with the list he claimed now showed 130 Communists (again with the list) and resorted to more name-calling, the words of lawyer Joseph Nye Welch—"Have you no sense of decency, sir, at long last?"—drew thunderous applause in the chamber. During the hearings, McCarthy's bullying tactics also became the focus of two editions of Edward R. Murrow's influential *See It Now* news program, and when McCarthy appeared on the show to defend himself, he (wait for it) accused Murrow of working with Russian agents, and generally came off as a nut.

On December 2, 1954, a bipartisan group of sixty-seven senators censured McCarthy for his behavior, signaling the end of his career was near. (In Eisenhower's words, McCarthyism was now "McCarthywasm.") He died in office on May 2, 1957, from hepatitis, a result of the severe alcoholism that may have helped fuel his paranoia.

James Joyce's Ulysses

LOCATION: *United States* | TIME FRAME: *1920s–1930s*

WITH ITS MASSIVE LENGTH, STREAM-OF-CONSCIOUSNESS STYLE, AND HUNDREDS OF OBSCURE REFERENCES, *ULYSSES* HAS TERRIFIED MANY A FRESHMAN ENGLISH MAJOR. PARTS OF THE NOVEL PROVED EVEN MORE TERRIFYING TO GOVERNMENT CENSORS.

Irish novelist James Joyce was already an important writer (with *Dubliners* and *A Portrait of the Artist as a Young Man* under his belt) when he started publishing excerpts from *Ulysses*. The novel follows its protagonist, Leopold Bloom, through Dublin on one fairly uneventful day, loosely paralleling his adventures with incidents from Homer's *Odyssey*.

Joyce wrote *Ulysses* from 1914 to 1921, and initially published it as an eighteen-episode serial in literary journals. In America, it appeared in Margaret Anderson's magazine *The Little Review*—well, until the thirteenth installment resulted in an obscenity prosecution. The chapter described Bloom watching

---

SYLVIA BEACH, THE OWNER OF SHAKESPEARE AND COMPANY, A FAMOUS ENGLISH-LANGUAGE BOOKSTORE IN PARIS WHERE JAMES WAS A FREQUENT VISITOR, WAS THE FIRST TO PUBLISH *ULYSSES* IN ITS ENTIRETY.

---

a young woman from afar, fantasizing about her and pleasuring himself. The scene ticked off the New York Society for the Suppression of Vice, which immediately set about suppressing Joyce's prose. The group won a 1921 obscenity ruling against the magazine, effectively banning *Ulysses* in the United States.

JOYCE'S NATIVE IRELAND NEVER CENSORED *ULYSSES*— AT LEAST NOT AS A BOOK. THE 1967 MOVIE VERSION STARRING MILO O'SHEA WAS BANNED IN THE EMERALD ISLE FOR THIRTY-THREE YEARS AS "SUBVERSIVE TO PUBLIC MORALITY" BEFORE A NEW CENSOR REMOVED THE PROHIBITION IN 2000.

WHY THE PANIC? Credit for lifting the ban in America goes to Random House, which forced the issue by trying to import the French edition of the now-completed novel in 1933. Customs officials seized the books, Random House contested the seizure, and the case went to court. On December 6, a district court judge ruled that Joyce's work was not pornographic in nature, and therefore not obscene. An appellate court confirmed that ruling, and struck a major blow against literary censorship in the United States by rejecting the notion that what would corrupt a "vulnerable child" was the proper standard for determining whether a work was obscene. (The ruling even conceded that most of the great works of literature could be deemed obscene under the existing standard.)

The U.S. Supreme Court later rejected the "vulnerable child" standard, ruling in a 1952 case that a work had to be "utterly without redeeming social importance" as well as appealing to "prurient interests" in order to be considered obscene. By that point, Americans had been able to read *Ulysses* for more than twenty years, and—considering how tough a read it is—some were probably still working on it.

Lady Chatterley's Lover

LOCATION: *Global* | TIME FRAME: *1920s–1950s*

NOT ONLY DID *LADY CHATTERLEY'S LOVER* DEMONSTRATE THE OLD AXIOM THAT SEX SELLS, BUT IT ALSO PROVED THAT GOVERNMENT CENSORSHIP COULD TURN A LITERARY WORK INTO A REALLY ENTICING PIECE OF FORBIDDEN FRUIT.

First published in Italy in 1928, D. H. Lawrence's novel centers on a wealthy noblewoman who starts a relationship with a working-class gamekeeper. Lawrence's sexually explicit descriptions of the affair—and his use of several words you still can't say on network TV—caused an instant sensation, and the book sold all of its limited-release copies. While several publishers around the world published a heavily "cleaned-up" version, governments from the United States to Japan blocked the release of the unabridged text. That made pirate versions all the more in demand.

In the United States, a 1930 amendment to the Smoot-Hawley Tariff Act took the role of censoring obscene material away from the customs office and gave it to the court system. (Senator Smoot himself threatened to read salacious

> NOT ONLY WAS LAWRENCE'S BOOK BANNED FOR A TIME IN AUSTRALIA, BUT SO WAS A 1961 NONFICTION ACCOUNT OF THE BRITISH OBSCENITY TRIAL BY C. H. ROLPH.

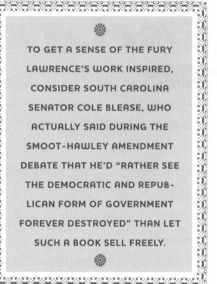

TO GET A SENSE OF THE FURY
LAWRENCE'S WORK INSPIRED,
CONSIDER SOUTH CAROLINA
SENATOR COLE BLEASE, WHO
ACTUALLY SAID DURING THE
SMOOT-HAWLEY AMENDMENT
DEBATE THAT HE'D "RATHER SEE
THE DEMOCRATIC AND REPUB-
LICAN FORM OF GOVERNMENT
FOREVER DESTROYED" THAN LET
SUCH A BOOK SELL FREELY.

passages from the book on the Senate floor. He didn't follow through.) The prohibition on books deemed pornographic survived even after American courts struck down other restrictions on published work. So in 1959, Grove Press tried printing an unexpurgated *Lady Chatterley*, and the resulting court case overturned an obscenity ban on the book.

WHY THE PANIC? When the British Parliament passed a new Obscene Publications Act in 1959—one that let publishers avoid punishment if they could prove a work had actual literary merit—*Lady Chatterley* seemed a perfect test case. Penguin Books tried to release an unexpurgated version, and the trial that followed forever changed British censorship. The prosecution's argument hung on notions of public decency, asking, "Is it a book you would even wish your wife or your servants to read?" Jurors apparently thought so, finding Penguin not guilty. All the pent-up demand exploded once the full *Lady Chatterley* was readily available—all two hundred thousand available copies sold out on the first day of legal UK publication.

The book sold more than two million copies in Britain within the first year, and was generally credited with helping inspire the 1960s sexual revolution there and in North America. Unfortunately, all that success came too late for Lawrence, who died in 1930.

Go Ask Alice

LOCATION: *North America* | TIME FRAME: *1971*

SORT OF A NEW *REEFER MADNESS* AIMED AT THE HIPPIE GENERATION, *GO ASK ALICE* BRIEFLY CAUSED A SENSATION WITH ITS MESSAGE THAT DROPPING ACID WAS THE GATEWAY TO A LIFE OF INEVITABLE WANTON DEPRAVITY.

The controversial book came out in 1971, when the psychedelic era was still in full force and parents of teenagers were more than willing to buy a book warning their kids not to turn on and drop out. *Alice* presented itself as the diary of an unnamed teenage girl (the author was listed as "Anonymous") who tries LSD for the first time after moving to a new town. As she spends more time with her new, drug-using friends, the narrator starts experimenting with more narcotics and loses her virginity while high.

Before long, she runs away from home twice, gets sexually assaulted, trades sex for drugs, goes to rehab, hitchhikes in dangerous areas, and loses pretty much all her friends. A postscript reports that three weeks after she

---

THE BOOK'S TITLE WAS INSPIRED BY A PHRASE IN THE TRIPPY JEFFERSON AIRPLANE TRACK "WHITE RABBIT," ITSELF INSPIRED BY LEWIS CARROLL'S TRIPPY *ALICE'S ADVENTURES IN WONDERLAND*. THE AUTHOR OF THE DIARY IS NEVER IDENTIFIED AS ALICE.

finished her diary, claiming she had cleaned up and was no longer in need of writing about her mistakes, she died of an overdose.

> ❋
>
> ODDLY, A MORALIZING BOOK CREATED SPECIFICALLY TO SCARE KIDS AWAY FROM DRUGS HAS ALSO SCARED MORALIZING PARENTS INTO BANNING IT FROM SCHOOL LIBRARIES (BASED ON ITS LANGUAGE AND DEPICTIONS OF SEX AND DRUGS). BANS STARTED IN MICHIGAN IN THE 1970S, AND *ALICE* CONTINUES TO RANK AMONG THE MOST-CHALLENGED BOOKS EVEN TODAY.
>
> ❋

THE AFTERMATH If it seems too much to be true, that's because it was. *Alice* was copyrighted by Beatrice Sparks, a Mormon youth counselor who later claimed the book was based on the diary of one of her patients (though she was unable to produce that diary). And while the book was written in the style of a diary with daily entries, the obviously planned narrative arc and contrived plot clearly made it a fictional work. Sparks even admitted she added a number of incidents to the alleged original diary. That didn't stop the book from staying in print to this day and selling more than four million copies, or from being adapted into a movie (with William Shatner playing the narrator's father and Andy Griffith her priest).

The "real diary" device worked well for Sparks, who went on to write a whole serious of cautionary tales for teenagers in the same style. They included *Jay's Journal* (which dealt with satanic cults), *It Happened to Nancy* (HIV/AIDS), and *Kim: Empty Inside* (eating disorders).

Parental Advisory Sticker

LOCATION: *United States* | TIME FRAME: *1980s*

THE BLACK-AND-WHITE "PARENTAL ADVISORY" STICKER ON THE FRONT OF AN ALBUM HAS BECOME SUCH A NORMAL SIGHT THAT YOUNG WHIPPERSNAPPERS MIGHT BE FORGIVEN FOR NOT REALIZING HOW BIG A DEAL THE FIGHT OVER THESE STICKERS WAS BACK IN THE DAY.

An advisory sticker was the brainchild of the Parents Music Resource Center, a group formed in 1985 by a quartet of prominent political wives. Tipper Gore, then-wife of then-senator and future vice president Al Gore, reportedly got the idea after listening to the Prince song "Darling Nikki" with her daughter and being unpleasantly surprised by the sexually explicit lyrics. The experience inspired her to check out MTV, where she found more music and videos she deemed offensive. Being a Washington insider, her first instinct was to form a committee, and so the PMRC was born.

The PMRC wasn't the first group to ask the Recording Industry Association of America

> THE PMRC RELEASED A "FILTHY FIFTEEN" LIST OF OFFENSIVE SONGS, INCLUDING CYNDI LAUPER'S "SHE BOP," DEF LEPPARD'S "HIGH AND DRY," TWISTED SISTER'S "WE'RE NOT GONNA TAKE IT," AND JUDAS PRIEST'S "EAT ME ALIVE."

to warn parents about explicit content. In fact, the National Parent Teacher Association had requested exactly that in October 1984 when it asked thirty record labels to voluntarily use stickers—only to get shot down thirty times. With its D.C. connections, however, the PMRC was able to get a high-profile Senate hearing on controversial lyrics.

> ❈
> ZAPPA BECAME THE STAR OF THE WHOLE AFFAIR (WHICH HE DUBBED "AN ILL-CONCEIVED PIECE OF NONSENSE"). AS A "REWARD," HIS *JAZZ FROM HELL* ALBUM GOT AN "EXPLICIT LYRICS" STICKER—EVEN THOUGH IT WAS AN INSTRUMENTAL ALBUM WITH NO LYRICS.
> ❈

WHY THE PANIC? While pressure from the PMRC and its allies had already prompted nineteen labels to agree to use a parental advisory sticker by the summer of 1985, the hearings that September made national news and featured big-name musicians John Denver, Frank Zappa, and Twisted Sister's Dee Snider testifying against the sticker.

The PMRC won a big victory on November 1 when, before the hearings were even over, the RIAA agreed to place the now-ubiquitous "Parental Advisory: Explicit Lyrics" sticker on potentially controversial albums. Of course, because it's up to the record companies to label their own albums, there have been oodles of abnormalities—with some seemingly innocuous records getting the sticker and others with "mature content" getting away without it. (Albums released earlier than 1985 mostly manage to avoid retroactive labeling.) While Wal-Mart and a few other retailers refuse to stock anything with the "Tipper Sticker," the warning has ironically become a badge of honor for artists who want to make clear they aren't parent-approved.

Nancy Reagan's "Just Say No" Campaign

LOCATION: *United States* | TIME FRAME: *1980s*

IF YOU GREW UP IN THE 1980S, ODDS ARE YOU ATTENDED AT LEAST ONE SCHOOL ASSEMBLY URGING YOU TO "JUST SAY NO" WHEN HIGH-PRESSURE PUSHERS INEVITABLY CORNERED YOU WITH FREE SAMPLES OF ADDICTIVE GATEWAY DRUGS.

For that, you can partly thank Nancy Reagan, who became the public face of the "Just Say No" antidrug campaign during her husband's presidency. The campaign was actually a spin-off of a 1970s National Institutes of Health program that aimed to fight childhood drug use by teaching kids how to reject peer pressure. The "Just Say No" name, however, was inspired by Mrs. Reagan's 1982 visit to an Oakland elementary school, and her answer to a child's question about what to do when offered drugs.

The simple slogan caught on, and soon the green-and-white

> IN ITS HEYDAY, "JUST SAY NO" WAS JUST ONE OF MANY SIMILAR PROGRAMS, INCLUDING WINNERS DON'T USE DRUGS, DRUG ABUSE RESISTANCE EDUCATION (D.A.R.E.), ABOVE THE INFLUENCE, ALERT PLUS, AND DOZENS OF OTHERS THAT WORKED TO DIMINISH TOBACCO, ALCOHOL, AND DRUG USE AMONG KIDS.

"Just Say No" logo was popping up all over. So was Nancy. The first lady hit the road regularly in support of the campaign, claiming to have traveled 250,000 miles on its behalf. The former star of *Hellcats of the Navy* and *Donovan's Brain* also appeared as herself on shows like *Diff'rent Strokes* and *Designing Women*, while making dozens of talk-show appearances in support of "Just Say No." She even wound up costarring with the likes of La Toya Jackson, Casey Kasem, and Kareem Abdul-Jabbar in a 1985 antidrug music video (which didn't exactly crack the Top 40). That same year, she hosted a high-profile conference on drug abuse in Washington, featuring an all-star team of first ladies from thirty nations.

THE AFTERMATH Whether all that effort made a difference is, of course, open to debate. Critics charged that the campaign's approach was actually far too simple; or that it didn't focus enough on serious drug abuse, didn't address underlying social issues, and cost quite a bit. Supporters cited "Just Say No" as one reason drug use among students dropped considerably by the end of the decade—though even they acknowledge there were a lot of other factors (from high-profile overdose deaths like that of basketball star Len Bias to cocaine use naturally falling after an all-time peak). Say this for Nancy Reagan, though— she stayed involved. After leaving the White House, she established an eponymous foundation and after-school program focused on substance abuse, and continued to give speeches on the subject for years.

Satanic Ritual Abuse

LOCATION: *North America* | TIME FRAME: *1980s*

THE CONCEPT OF SATAN GOES BACK TO THE OLD TESTAMENT, AND STORIES OF DEMONIC POSSESSION TRACE BACK TO AT LEAST THE MIDDLE AGES. BUT THE 1980S SAW A BIZARRE SPIKE IN TALES OF DEVIL WORSHIPPERS TORTURING AND ABUSING UNSUSPECTING KIDS.

Looking back, the era looks like a perfect cauldron for brewing satanic conspiracies. A strain of Christianity that believed in the literal reality of the devil was on the rise, recent years had seen several cults do serious damage, and the idea of bringing up repressed memories through hypnosis was just catching on. So the time was right for a moral panic about satanic ritual abuse (or SRA).

Two much-publicized incidents drove the SRA panic. First was the 1980 publication of *Michelle Remembers*. Written by Michelle Smith and her psychiatrist (and future husband)

> AS FURTHER "EVIDENCE" OF SATANIC GOINGS-ON, *MICHELLE REMEMBERS* CITED THE CASE OF EVANGELIST LEN OLSEN, WHO'D CLAIMED THAT SATANISTS TRIED TO SACRIFICE HIM AND HIS WIFE. IT LEFT OUT THAT OLSEN HAD ALREADY LOST A DEFAMATION CASE OVER HIS COMMENTS, AND THAT HIS DELUSIONS WERE BLAMED ON DRUG USE.

Lawrence Pazder, the book included Smith's supposedly repressed memories—brought out during hypnosis by Pazder—of being abused by a satanic cult when she was five. Pazder used the book to launch a career consulting in cases of SRA (a term he coined), and claimed to have worked on a thousand cases by 1990.

THE PINNACLE Then there was the 1983 McMartin preschool trial in California, in which a teacher and an administrator were accused of abusing children. A social worker who interviewed hundreds of the preschool's children and relied on leading questions got many to describe satanic rituals and bizarre abuse (like Chuck Norris abusing them, or children being flushed down toilets). The defendants were acquitted (and the mother who launched the initial allegations was diagnosed with schizophrenia and alcoholism), but the three-year-long trial got a lot of coverage.

While the McMartin trial was still going on, the social worker involved warned a congressional committee that a worldwide satanic conspiracy was forcing kids to watch animal and human sacrifice. More psychiatrists reported bringing out memories of these rituals through hypnosis, and tabloid shows featured reports on the satanic panic.

By about 1986, however, media coverage of ritual abuse focused more on why hypnosis and leading questions were inherently unreliable, and several lawsuits against psychiatrists who pushed the satanic abuse theory helped end the panic.

Dungeons & Dragons

LOCATION: *North America* | TIME FRAME: *1980s*

SURE, DUNGEONS & DRAGONS MIGHT BE DETRIMENTAL TO ONE'S ABILITY TO TALK TO GIRLS. BUT FOR A STRETCH OF TIME IN THE 1980S, SOME FEARED THE ROLE-PLAYING PHENOMENON WAS ALSO DETRIMENTAL TO ONE'S ABILITY TO AVOID MURDERING ONE'S FRIENDS, OR ONESELF.

While it's gone through many incarnations, D&D is essentially a role-playing game in which players choose personas from a range of classic fantasy characters—wizard, thief, barbarian—go on "adventures" narrated by a "Dungeon Master," and use dice rolls to determine the outcomes of their actions. The game debuted in 1974, and by 1980 was a big hit with gamers. Nerdy? Definitely. Dangerous? Hardly. Then several kids who played the game committed suicide, and D&D became something handy to blame.

THE PINNACLE The case that really caused a frenzy was the 1982 suicide of Virginia teenager Bink Pulling. He obviously had a number of problems—the kid

> THE ISRAELI ARMY HAS AN OFFICIAL POLICY TO GIVE LOWER SECURITY CLEARANCE TO RECRUITS WHO PLAY D&D OR SIMILAR GAMES, CLAIMING THEY ARE "DETACHED FROM REALITY AND SUSCEPTIBLE TO INFLUENCE."

had made a habit of mutilating rabbits, for example—but his mother blamed the suicide on his playing D&D at school and claimed a "curse" his character acquired during a game was the final straw. Patricia Pulling sued TSR (the company behind the game) and her son's school (where he played it), claiming they were responsible for Bink's death—ignoring that he killed himself with her gun. When both lawsuits failed, she started an advocacy group against role-playing games, forming Bothered About Dungeons & Dragons (BADD).

> PULLING ONCE DESCRIBED D&D AS PUSHING "DEMONOLOGY, WITCH-CRAFT, VOODOO, MURDER, RAPE, BLASPHEMY, SUICIDE, ASSASSINA-TION, INSANITY, SEX PERVERSION, HOMOSEXUALITY, PROSTITUTION, SATANIC-TYPE RITUALS, GAM-BLING, BARBARISM, CANNIBALISM, SADISM, DESECRATION, DEMON SUMMONING, NECROMANTICS, DIVINATION AND OTHER TEACH-INGS." BUT ASIDE FROM THAT . . .

Pulling used BADD to generate negative publicity about the game, claiming its fantasy-based stories drew kids to the occult and citing D&D as the cause anytime a teen known to play it committed suicide. While there were only a few cases of gamers killing themselves—and none in which the game was a clear cause—that didn't stop the self-proclaimed "cult crime expert." Several conservative Christian groups also took up the cause. At the peak of the panic, even *60 Minutes* got interested, airing a 1985 segment on the alleged connection.

By the end of the 1980s, though, a series of news reports clearly debunked BADD's arguments. While the panic eventually died down, D&D's popularity continued. The company estimates that more than 20 million people have played the game—and lived to tell about it.

Heavy Metal Suicide

LOCATION: *North America* | TIME FRAME: *1980s*

O NE SUREFIRE WAY TO SPARK A MORAL PANIC IN 1980S AMERICA WAS TO GET BLAMED FOR A TEEN SUICIDE—WHICH IS HOW HEAVY METAL JOINED THE RATHER LONG LIST OF SCAPEGOATS.

By the start of the decade, heavy metal music had thoroughly embraced its dark side, as bands like Black Sabbath, Judas Priest, and Iron Maiden effectively paired devilish imagery with increasingly hard-driving sounds. The formula worked, as sales were good and metal provided an edgier alternative to the New Wave and pop scenes.

The dark imagery made metal a popular target for Christian groups and censorship movements, but things got really out of hand in 1985. That December in Reno, friends Raymond Belknap and James Vance made a murder-suicide pact—while drunk and high, by the way. The twenty-year-old

> PARODY ACTS LOVED THE IDEA OF SONGS WITH HIDDEN MESSAGES. ONE "WEIRD AL" YANKOVIC SONG PLAYED BACKWARD SAYS, "WOW, YOU MUST HAVE AN AWFUL LOT OF FREE TIME ON YOUR HANDS," WHILE A TRACK BY JACK BLACK'S TENACIOUS D ORDERS LISTENERS TO "EAT DONKEY CRAP."

Vance killed Belknap with a shotgun, then shot himself. Vance survived, horribly disfigured, but died a few years later from surgery-related complications.

During that gap, Vance—also a serious drug addict—wrote a letter claiming, "I believe that alcohol and heavy-metal music, such as Judas Priest, led us or even 'mesmerized' us into believing that the answer to 'life was death.'" So his parents decided Judas Priest was at fault for the whole thing and sued the band, claiming there was a subliminal message in the band's song "Better by You Better by Me." The alleged message allegedly said, "Do it," though there was really nothing to suggest "it" meant suicide. Judas Priest maintained it never recorded any subliminal messages at all, and the members all made a point of testifying at the 1990 civil trial.

> THE BEST ONE-LINER OF THE TRIAL BELONGED TO JUDAS PRIEST SINGER ROB HALFORD, WHO SUGGESTED THAT IF THE BAND WERE TO USE A SUBLIMINAL MESSAGE, IT WOULD BE "BUY MORE OF OUR RECORDS." HE ALSO POINTED OUT THAT URGING FANS WHO BUY RECORDS TO KILL THEMSELVES WOULD BE RATHER COUNTERPRODUCTIVE.

THE AFTERMATH The courts dismissed the case, but the trial inspired its share of copycats. Just a few months after Judas Priest's legal victory, a teen shooting himself while listening to Ozzy Osbourne's *Suicide Solution* album prompted another (equally unsuccessful) lawsuit, and concerned parent groups got in the habit of listening to metal albums for subliminal or backward-playing messages. (More recently, during a 1996 congressional hearing, Marilyn Manson was blamed for another teen suicide.) While none of the cited songs actually had hidden lyrics, the discussion of them inspired other metal acts to start adding secret messages for their fans to find.

Rainbow Parties

LOCATION: *United States* | TIME FRAME: *2000s*

THOSE WACKY TEENAGERS. STUFFING THEMSELVES INTO PHONE BOOTHS. SWALLOWING GOLDFISH. THROWING ORAL-SEX PARTIES . . . WAIT, WHAT ABOUT THAT LAST ONE?

Sometime in the early 2000s, rumors started about Rainbow Parties. Supposedly, these were very specific orgies where teenagers got together to have massive amounts of oral sex. As for the "Rainbow" in the title, cover the little ones' eyes for a moment. The girls at these parties were said to wear different colors of lipstick and leave a ring of colors on the boys' penises. If a guy enjoyed the party enough, he would theoretically wind up decorated with all the colors of the rainbow. (With seven colors in the rainbow, he'd also wind up exhausted.)

These parties were either an urban legend or a rare phenomenon blown out of proportion. However, if you've ever doubted the power of Oprah Winfrey,

> THE SEX-DRIVEN RAINBOW PARTIES ARE NOT TO BE CONFUSED WITH GREECE'S RAINBOW PARTY, WHICH IS A REGIONAL POLITICAL PARTY DEVOTED TO CIVIL RIGHTS FOR THE COUNTRY'S MACEDONIAN MINORITY. ENOUGH PEOPLE CONFUSED THEM, THOUGH, TO DRIVE UP THE POLITICAL PARTY'S WEB TRAFFIC.

consider what happened next. In a 2003 episode of her show about teen promiscuity, a guest—an editor at Oprah's *O Magazine*—described Rainbow Parties as a growing trend among teens. Suddenly parents started asking their kids about Rainbow Parties, and they started to seem like a real trend. In the words of researcher Deborah Tolman, "One day we have never heard of Rainbow Parties, and then suddenly they are everywhere, feeding on adults' fears that morally bankrupt sexuality among teens is rampant, despite any actual evidence." That, folks, is a classic moral panic.

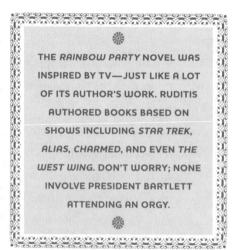

THE *RAINBOW PARTY* NOVEL WAS INSPIRED BY TV—JUST LIKE A LOT OF ITS AUTHOR'S WORK. RUDITIS AUTHORED BOOKS BASED ON SHOWS INCLUDING *STAR TREK*, *ALIAS*, *CHARMED*, AND EVEN *THE WEST WING*. DON'T WORRY; NONE INVOLVE PRESIDENT BARTLETT ATTENDING AN ORGY.

THE PINNACLE The idea got a further boost in 2005, with the publication of the novel *Rainbow Party* by Paul Ruditis. While fiction, it was a story about teenagers fantasizing about having an orgy not unlike the ones discussed on *Oprah*—which was fitting considering an editor at Simon & Schuster admitted getting the idea after watching the *Oprah* episode. The book was theoretically supposed to serve as a cautionary tale, but the publicity added to the pop-culture notion that this probable urban legend was a real trend; an informal *New York Times* survey at the time found a majority of teen girls were familiar with the idea of Rainbow Parties, even if they never attended one (or found them gross). While more people knew of them, there was no sign that more of these parties were actually happening, and the fears about them soon died down.

Sexting

LOCATION: *Global* | TIME FRAME: *2000s*

WITH THE INTERNET, PEOPLE TOOK AN EXCITING NEW TECHNOLOGY THAT OFFERED EASY ACCESS TO THE COLLECTIVE KNOWLEDGE OF THE WORLD AND TURNED IT INTO A VEHICLE FOR DELIVERING PORN. SO IT WAS ONLY A MATTER OF TIME BEFORE THE SAME TREND MADE ITS WAY TO CELL PHONES.

The term "sexting" dates to at least 2005, and became the accepted shorthand for the growing trend of using mobile phones to send sexually explicit text messages. And the introduction of the standard-issue camera phone (with 50 million in use in America by 2005) only fanned the flames. Texters quickly decided messages with visual aids were sexier, and sexting soon became a way to send personalized porn to a significant other or potential partner.

Of course, cell phones keep records, and photos intended for private viewing could go public in a big way. The Disney Channel learned that the hard way when hackers got ahold of racy photos that two of its wholesome stars—

BY 2006, NEARLY 80 PERCENT OF NEW CELL PHONES CAME WITH A BUILT-IN CAMERA. NOT COINCIDENTALLY, THAT'S THE YEAR SEXTING REALLY TOOK OFF.

High School Musical's Vanessa Hudgens and *Hannah Montana*'s Miley Cyrus— had texted to their boyfriends. Golf star Tiger Woods saw his rather graphic sex talk with dozens of mistresses become fodder for late-night comedians, while photos of NBA center Greg Oden in all his glory found their way online. Just a few weeks after winning an Academy Award, Sandra Bullock divorced her husband, whose "sexts" with a heavily tattooed fetish model had become a public scandal.

WHY THE PANIC? Aside from the potential for embarrassment, there was another obvious problem with the trend. Texting was particularly popular with teenagers, so, when they started sexting, they were by definition producing and distributing child pornography. And having the images or videos on a phone made distribution really easy, as a scorned ex or jealous rival could quickly convert a teen's best-forgotten memories into viewing fodder for creepy porn enthusiasts around the world.

Concerned adults responded by trying to punish sexters through legal means. In 2007 alone, thirty-two teenagers in the Australian state of Victoria were prosecuted on child-pornography charges. In Pennsylvania, six teens faced similar child-porn charges in early 2009 after a teacher confiscated a disruptive student's phone, found nude images, and prompted a police investigation that unearthed more phones with compromising pictures. An unfortunate school official in Virginia even faced charges for possession of child porn because his principal asked him to save a confiscated nude photo of a student as evidence (he was cleared of wrongdoing after an expensive process). With sexting now a reality of the times, a few state governments—including those of Ohio, Vermont, and Utah—have debated laws to lessen the punishments for underage sexters, as long as it's consensual.

Chapter 4

Fashion Fads

FROM THE TIME EARLY MAN FIRST STARTED DRESSING IN FURS, SOMEBODY'S ALWAYS COME ALONG WITH A WAY TO STAND OUT FROM THE CROWD. Then everyone in the crowd copies their look, and we get a full-on fashion trend. Some fads come to define their eras (bobbed hair); a few have staying power long after their peak (miniskirts), and others remain embarrassing relics stashed in the back of a closet or popping up in compromising photos (parachute pants or the male perm). Here are some of the fashions that made it huge before becoming *so* last year.

Bobbed Hair

TO GET A SENSE OF HOW INFLUENTIAL "THE BOB" HAIRCUT WAS, CONSIDER THAT BEFORE THE 1920S, MOST HAIR SALONS CATERED *EXCLUSIVELY* TO MEN, WHILE WOMEN JUST LET THEIR LOCKS GROW OUT. BY THE TIME F. SCOTT FITZGERALD CELEBRATED THE STYLE IN HIS POPULAR 1920 STORY "BERNICE BOBS HER HAIR," A GENERATION OF WOMEN HAD MADE SHORT HAIR SHORTHAND FOR A WHOLE NEW APPROACH TO FASHION.

❀

LIKE ANY SUDDEN, SWEEPING CHANGE, THE BOB HAD ITS SHARE OF DETRACTORS. IN 1925, A NEW JERSEY SCHOOLTEACHER WAS ORDERED BY HER LOCAL EDUCATION BOARD TO KEEP HER HAIR LONG, AND THERE WERE REPORTS OF STORES FIRING BOB-HAIRED WOMEN EN MASSE.

❀

The bob cut allegedly started among World War I working women who quite understandably wanted to keep their long hair from getting caught in dangerous machinery. As far as a chic style goes, though, it began with Irene Castle, a famous ballroom dancer whose 1915 decision to cut her hair to about the length of her ears gained widespread attention.

WHY THE FAD? It only helped the popularity of the bob that it came along at a time when women's fashion was undergoing a complete overhaul. The whole "flapper" ethos saw women becoming more independent and dressing in that spirit with higher hemlines and long cigarette holders. The bob worked nicely with the flapper aesthetic, and with the Art Deco–inspired cloche hats that were coming into vogue. Fashion icons like designer Coco Chanel and actress Clara Bow started chopping off their hair, and once enough women were convinced that short hair wasn't suddenly going to go out of style, thousands and thousands followed suit.

> ✽
>
> BOBBY PINS WERE SO NAMED FOR THEIR USEFULNESS IN KEEPING BOBBED HAIR IN PLACE, THOUGH THEY HAD ALREADY BEEN IN USE FOR MANY YEARS.
>
> ✽

In a span of five years, the number of hairdressing shops in America reportedly jumped from five thousand to twenty-one thousand, with women taking over as the main clientele. Bobbed hair branched out into a number of new looks, including the flatter Dutch Boy bob, bobs with waves and curls, and the even shorter "Eton Crop" that left the ears totally exposed.

Unlike most fashion trends that grew as quickly, bobbed hair has stayed popular. There have been dozens of variations since the 1920s, but bobbed hair is so common today that it seems weird that it seemed weird not all that long ago.

Male Perm

LOCATION: *United States* | TIME FRAME: *1970s–1980s*

WHAT DO MICHAEL JACKSON, PRINCE, RICK JAMES, DEBARGE, AND MOST OF NEW EDITION HAVE IN COMMON? NO, NOT JUST THE HIT RECORDS. AT SOME POINT IN THE 1980S, EACH AND EVERY ONE FELL VICTIM TO THE TREND OF THE JHERI CURL, THE BRIEFLY UBIQUITOUS MALE PERM.

Particularly popular in the African-American community, the Jheri Curl and its less memorable competitors (including Luster Curls and Carefree Curls) allowed men to have long, stringy curls that looked more like a glob of seaweed than natural hair. That was just one of the drawbacks. Keeping the curls in place involved an exhaustive daily routine. First men had to apply a softening cream to loosen the hair, and then another chemical solution that curled and set the hair, as well as a routine application of moisturizers and "activators" to keep the curl in place throughout the day. Not surprisingly, treating hair with that many chemicals often left it dry, coarse, and brittle—which only created more of a reason to perm it. The easy availability and generally low cost of the

IN RARE CASES, THE PERM COULD EVEN GET DANGEROUS—THE CHEMICAL MIXTURE IS LARGELY BLAMED FOR MICHAEL JACKSON'S HAIR CATCHING FIRE DURING THE FILMING OF A DOOMED PEPSI COMMERCIAL.

treatments helped the Jheri Curl trend spread, because men could give themselves a perm at home rather than constantly go to a salon. But while these perms were widely advertised as convenient "wash-and-wear" styles, the actual upkeep could take nearly as many hours as a moonlighting job.

WHY THE FAD? The Jheri Curl formula owes its creation to Jheri Redding, one of the godfathers of American hair care. The Chicago-based inventor, best known for creating the "crème rinse" we now just call "conditioner," also brought us pH-balanced shampoo and various hair colors, while also founding or cofounding companies like Nexxus, Jhirmack, and Redken. So the "underground" Jheri Curl look was in reality the product of a major player.

❋

AN OBVIOUS DOWNSIDE TO THE CHEMICAL CONCOCTION WAS HOW EASILY IT RUBBED OFF ON PILLOWS, CLOTHING, OR UPHOLSTERY, FORCING MEN TO SLEEP WITH A PLASTIC CAP ON THEIR HEADS OR DO LAUNDRY A LOT MORE REGULARLY. PERMED MEN UNINTENTIONALLY COMMITTED COUNTLESS PARTY FOULS BY LEANING BACK ON A FRIEND'S COUCH AND LEAVING A GREASY CHEMICAL MIX BEHIND.

❋

While the popularity of the male perm faded by the end of the 1980s and virtually died out by the early 1990s, Redding continued a long and successful career until he (and his straight hair) died in 1998 at the age of ninety-one.

Velcro Sneakers

LOCATION: *Global* | TIME FRAME: *1980s*

MAYBE IT WAS THE LOOK. OR A FONDNESS FOR THE DISTINCTIVE TEARING SOUND. OR A BURNING DESIRE TO AVOID SPENDING PRECIOUS SECONDS TYING THOSE PESKY LACES. WHATEVER THE REASON, VELCRO SHOES BECAME *THE* FOOTWEAR OF THE 1980S.

The phenomenon was a long time coming. Swiss inventor George de Mestral got the idea for Velcro in 1941, when he and his dog returned from a hike with clothes and fur covered in cockleburs. After studying the burs under a microscope, de Mestral noticed their small hooks made them strong fasteners. It took him a few tries to get the materials right, but by 1955, de Mestral had patented his two-sided, hook-and-loop system. He named it Velcro by smushing together the French words for "velvet" and "crochet."

DE MESTRAL MADE LITTLE MONEY AT FIRST, BUT CLEARED MILLIONS AFTER SELLING THE RIGHTS TO HIS INVENTION IN THE 1950S.

"Velcro," like Xerox or Kleenex, soon became the colloquial term for any hook-and-loop fastener. And once de Mestral's patent expired in 1978, the market was flooded with lots of versions of the same basic product. By lucky coincidence, that happened around the same time sneakers started to take over as everyday shoes. For decades, athletic shoes were worn mostly by athletes (obviously) or just as activity-specific gear. As the 1980s rolled around, it wasn't unusual to see businesspeople or celebrities wearing sneakers nowhere near the gym. That casual look provided the perfect opportunity for the convenient Velcro straps to take over.

THE PINNACLE And take over they did. Nearly all the major shoe brands joined the Velcro fad during its mid-1980s peak, from heavyweights, like Nike and Reebok, to smaller lines that were fads in their own right—like the shoes-with-pockets KangaROOS or L.A. Gear with its oversize tongues. While their popularity gradually died down by the end of the Reagan years, Velcro sneakers have never really gone away. Like many fads, they've become an everyday item, and their tearing sound is still heard in locker rooms throughout the world.

꜅ ✳ ꜆

WHILE PUMA BECAME THE FIRST SHOE COMPANY TO MAKE FOOTWEAR WITH THE STUFF IN 1968, VELCRO WAS BETTER KNOWN AT THE TIME FOR ITS CONNECTION WITH THE SPACE PROGRAM. AFTER ALL, NASA WAS USING IT TO HOLD SPACESUITS TOGETHER, AND EVEN APPLIED IT LIKE CARPETING INSIDE SPACESHIPS TO KEEP ASTRONAUTS' PERSONAL STUFF FROM FLOATING AROUND IN ZERO GRAVITY. OVER TIME, VELCRO WAS ALSO RESPONSIBLE FOR HOLDING TOGETHER DOCTORS' BLOOD-PRESSURE CUFFS, TRAVEL WALLETS, AND EVEN AN ARTIFICIAL HUMAN HEART.

Uggs and Crocs

LOCATION: *North America* | TIME FRAME: *2000s*

IF ANYONE HAD PREDICTED THAT THE TWO BIGGEST FOOTWEAR TRENDS OF THE EARLY TWENTY-FIRST CENTURY WOULD INVOLVE AUSTRALIAN WORK BOOTS AND COLORFUL PLASTIC SHOES, FEW WOULD HAVE TAKEN THEM SERIOUSLY. OF COURSE, THOSE FEW WOULD NOW BE VERY, VERY RICH.

UGGS The sheepskin "ugg" boots date back to at least World War I, when Australian pilots used them to keep their feet warm in their poorly insulated aircraft. Their durability and comfort (due to the tough leather outside and soft wool inside) made them popular Down Under with farmers and surfers, though they were considered aesthetically ugly (hence the name).

That reputation didn't deter an American company from trademarking the Ugg name in the USA—and marketing the heck out of it to consumers, who responded like, well, sheep. By 2003, Oprah Winfrey was giving free pairs to her audience and actresses like Sarah Jessica Parker and Julia Roberts had taken to wearing them as an "antifashion" statement, which of course made them seem that much more fashionable. Before long, American

> THE POPULARITY OF UGGS STATESIDE HASN'T BEEN SO POPULAR BACK IN AUSTRALIA. THE SHEEPSKIN ASSOCIATION THERE ESTIMATED THE TRADEMARKING OF "UGG" COST THE INDUSTRY AT LEAST $20 MILLION BY PREVENTING OTHER COMPANIES FROM USING THE TERM.

women were ordering these shoes of Outback roughnecks in pink or powder blue, spending more than $300 to tuck their hipster skinny jeans into a pair.

CROCS Crocs lacked the historic pedigree and high price of Uggs but became the next unlikely trend to rival their popularity. Crocs Inc. introduced its colorful clogs in 2002, and the shoes had a few gimmicks in their favor. The company's proprietary resin material was designed to prevent odors (always a plus) and to conform to the wearer's feet for comfort. Crocs also instantly appealed to those who found sandals just a little too formal.

Crocs took off right away and raised more than $200 million when the company went public in 2006. In case the dozens of

> CROCS WERE PRETTY UGLY IN THEIR OWN RIGHT, WITH MAINSTREAM FASHION CRITICS USING PHRASES LIKE "HIDEOUS" AND "SPREADING LIKE VERMIN" TO DESCRIBE THE CLOGS. THE COMPANY EVEN ADMITTED AS MUCH, RUNNING A FAMOUS AD IN *VANITY FAIR* CLAIMING "UGLY CAN BE BEAUTIFUL."

available colors didn't make the shoes personal enough, Crocs introduced Jibbitz (a line of charm jewelry specifically made to decorate the shoes) and kept adding colors and patterns to the product line at a furious pace. Before long, there were Crocs heels, Crocs boots, Crocs flats, Crocs flip-flops—you get the idea. Unfortunately for the company, the fad started to fade almost as soon as it hit. By 2008, Crocs stock had taken a massive hit, and it had become a lot easier to go out in public without seeing dozens of the clogs. It started to look like there might be a limit to just how casually people wanted to dress, leaving investors wondering if the whole fad was a bit of a Croc.

Miniskirt

LOCATION: *Global* | TIME FRAME: *1960s*

FOR MORE THAN FOUR DECADES, THE MINISKIRT HAS BEEN THE RARE FASHION TREND THAT CLEARLY UNITES MEN AND WOMEN IN SUPPORT, ALBEIT FOR DIFFERENT REASONS.

Fans of both genders can thank London designer Mary Quant, who first began selling shorter skirts out of her Chelsea shop in the late 1950s. The year of the miniskirt was 1965, when Quant introduced the above-the-knee version that defined the miniskirt as we know it, French designer André Courrèges (later nicknamed "lord of the miniskirt") first added miniskirts into his "mod" line, and model Jean Shrimpton caused a sensation by showing a whole lot of leg at Australia's Melbourne Cup horse race. Few things underscored a generation gap in clothing better than photos of a fashionable Shrimpton standing out among a bunch of disapproving middle-aged women with big hats and pearls. Girls and young women took notice.

WHY THE FAD? That the miniskirt came from London gave it added cachet, because—between the "Swinging London" mod scene and the British Invasion that was dominating rock music—the United Kingdom had become the epicenter of youth culture worldwide. Courrèges also marketed his miniskirts as part of a "space age" look, at a time when the space race was still new and exciting.

Its ability to tick off the parents was only one reason the miniskirt (and its cousin, the minidress) became so popular. The material was easy to quickly wash and dry, which was surprisingly hard to find in women's fashion at the time, and fit the on-the-go era. The miniskirt also lent itself to all kinds of new accessories that would basically become the early sixties look. Vinyl go-go boots and zip-up knee boots, for example, wouldn't have worked with longer skirts. As miniskirt-wearing women didn't need garter belts anymore, designers introduced hundreds of new designs for stockings and tights. Some designers started incorporating see-through material into their miniskirts, so women had to put a little more thought into their underwear (and the same designers were glad to oblige with new colors and designs).

EARLY IN ITS EXISTENCE, THE MINISKIRT INSPIRED BANS IN A NUMBER OF COUNTRIES—SOME WHERE IT WAS SEEN AS INDECENT, OTHERS WHERE IT WAS SEEN AS GIVING PERVERTS AN EXCUSE TO TAKE ADVANTAGE OF WOMEN. THOSE FEARS SOON DIED DOWN IN MOST PLACES, BUT EVEN IN THE PAST DECADE, COUNTRIES AS DIVERSE AS POLAND, UGANDA, SERBIA, AND KENYA HAVE SEEN LAWMAKERS ATTEMPT TO PASS BANS AGAINST THE MINISKIRT.

The miniskirt craze died out by the end of the 1960s, when the antiwar and civil rights movements made mainstream youth culture a far more serious affair. While no longer the must-have outfit, though, the short skirt had long-term appeal. The miniskirt never went out of style, and has become a permanent fixture in the fashion world.

Parachute Pants

LOCATION: *Global* | TIME FRAME: *1980s–1990s*

AS BELL-BOTTOMS WERE TO DISCO, PARACHUTE PANTS WERE TO BREAK-DANCING AND DANCE-RAP. EVEN TODAY, IT'S HARD TO LOOK AT THE PUFFY, COLORFUL THREADS WITHOUT THINKING OF MC HAMMER DOING THE RUNNING MAN.

Early parachute pants were made from ripstop nylon, a material fittingly used in actual parachutes, as well as hot-air balloons, kites, tents, sails—pretty much anything that had to be light but sturdy and wind-resistant. Those might not seem like must-have qualities for pants, but at least parachute pants did start out with a practical reason for their existence. The pants were specifically designed for break dancing, which involved a lot of spinning, brushing against the ground, and other moves that would rip a lesser material to shreds. Also, the roomy upper-leg area saved dancers from chafing while practicing their moves.

> ❋
>
> HAMMER MIGHT TAKE THE MOST FLAK FOR MAKING PARACHUTE PANTS PASSÉ, BUT VANILLA ICE AND THE CAST OF *SAVED BY THE BELL* WERE JUST AS GUILTY OF TAKING THE TREND FROM HIP TO CHEESY.
>
> ❋

Once parachute pants went mainstream, the puffy look stayed while the materials (and purpose for the design) changed completely. By the early 1990s, it was more common to see dress slacks with a "parachute" look than the old nylon version. As the Hammers of the world soon faded into obscurity, so did their signature look.

Sagging Pants

LOCATION: *Global* | TIME FRAME: *1990s–2000s*

IT'S HARD TO PINPOINT PRECISELY WHEN TEENAGERS AND YOUNG ADULTS STARTED WEARING THEIR TROUSERS WELL BELOW THE WAIST, BUT BY THE MID-1990S THE LOW-RIDER LOOK HAD CLEARLY BECOME A THING.

Legend holds that the baggy trend began as homage to the prison system. Because belts and cords were usually banned in the pokey (lest they become weapons or suicide aids), prisoners' pants hung low. Prison uniforms also notoriously ran large, meaning smaller inmates wound up with *really* low pants. So anyone spending time in prison might not have seen London or France, but definitely saw their fellow prisoners' underpants. (Despite persistent rumors to the contrary, the low-ride look was *not* specifically a calling card for prisoners signaling their homosexuality.) Unlaced shoes also became part of the outfit, as shoelaces were a prison no-no because of the same strangling-prevention policy.

LIKE ANY YOUTH-BASED FASHION TREND, SAGGING PANTS HAVE CAUSED SOME BACKLASH FROM THE OLDER GENERATION. BILL COSBY FAMOUSLY RIPPED "PANTS DOWN AROUND THE CRACK." EVEN PRESIDENT OBAMA WEIGHED IN, SAYING, "SOME PEOPLE MIGHT NOT WANT TO SEE YOUR UNDERWEAR— AND I'M ONE OF THEM."

WHY THE FAD? While prisons inspired the look, it was hip-hop culture that took it mainstream. As rap music shifted from the more pop-influenced variety to the harder, gangster style of the early 1990s (less Vanilla Ice, more Ice Cube and Ice-T), hard-core artists wore their pants low—albeit belted—to flaunt their street cred. One degree of separation later and young fans were copying the look for mostly musical, rather than "municipal," reasons. The look inspired designer boxer companies to give customers a variety of patterns that bore no resemblance to the dull threads of standard-issue prison garb.

GANGSTER WANNABES WEREN'T THE ONLY ONES LOOKING FOR PANTS THAT SHOWED OFF THEIR MIDRIFFS, AS THE LATE 1990S AND EARLY 2000S SAW A REVIVAL OF LOW-RISE "HIP-HUGGER" JEANS (AND, UNFORTUNATELY, THE SIMULTANEOUS REVIVAL OF THE "MUFFINTOP" AND "COIN SLOT").

HIP-HUGGERS HAD BEEN INCREDIBLY POPULAR IN THE HIPPIE ERA, WITH JIMI HENDRIX, ROBERT PLANT, AND JANIS JOPLIN ALL BIG FANS, BUT THE LOOK HAD STARTED TO DIE OUT BY THE END OF THE DISCO DAYS OF THE LATE SEVENTIES. TEEN POP STARS LIKE BRITNEY SPEARS AND CHRISTINA AGUILERA DIDN'T HAVE MUCH IN COMMON WITH JIMI AND JANIS, BUT THEIR POPULARITY LED TO A NEW STYLE OF HIP-HUGGERS: LOW-RISE JEANS, WHICH BECAME VERY POPULAR WITH TEENS AND MADE HITS OF THE CHAIN STORES BEST KNOWN FOR THEM, LIKE ABERCROMBIE & FITCH AND AMERICAN EAGLE.

Ganguro

SURE, 1980S AMERICA BECAME FAMOUS FOR BIZARRE FASHION TRENDS, BUT THAT WAS NOTHING ON THE WEIRDNESS SCALE COMPARED TO 1990S JAPAN.

For just one example, take Ganguro. Literally meaning "blackface," it involves traditionally light-skinned, dark-haired Japanese girls taking themselves in the extreme opposite direction until they look like year-round Halloween enthusiasts out of a John Waters movie. Most popular in the 1990s and early 2000s, the look was generally considered a way for girls to rebel against the "accepted" Japanese beauty standard, or a way to express their individuality (admittedly, by doing the same thing a bunch of others were doing).

WHAT'S THE FAD? Ganguro girls start not just by tanning, but by tanning so the color is way too dark to ever be considered "tan." (Some girls spray it on, while others go for the tanning beds.) Then they add dark powder or bronzers to make the fake tan even darker. The look also requires changing hair color, first by bleaching and then by dyeing—with fluorescent yellow, fluorescent orange, and fluorescent pink among the most popular shades. (Less hard-core girls just go with a simpler white or blond look, or "cheat" by wearing brightly colored wigs instead of bleaching.)

But skin and hair are just part of the look. Ganguro also usually involves white lipstick, white makeup applied in huge "panda" circles around the whole eye, fake eyebrows, and glitter or stickers all over the girl's face. Clothes, naturally, are also a key part of the ensemble, with miniskirts, sarongs, and platform shoes all adding to the intentionally cartoony look.

THE AFTERMATH The trend isn't limited to Japan, as Ganguro girls have popped up in North America and the United Kingdom, where Western girls are trying to look like Japanese girls trying to look more like Western girls. While usually just seen as weird in the West, Ganguro has prompted charges of racism, both from Westerners concerned about the blackface and Japanese girls angry at the appropriation of their style.

❀

FOR THOSE FOR WHOM MERE GANGURO ISN'T EDGY ENOUGH, THE STYLE HAS ITS OWN SUBGENRES. THERE'S YAMANBA, NAMED AFTER AN EVIL HAG CHARACTER IN JAPANESE FOLKLORE SAID TO HAVE A SIMILAR LOOK. YAMANBA GIRLS WEAR THEIR WHITE MAKEUP ABOVE BUT NOT BELOW THEIR EYES, ALONG WITH BRIGHT CONTACT LENSES. ANOTHER GROUP, CALLED MANBA GIRLS, GOES WITH WHITE MAKEUP AROUND THEIR WHOLE EYE BUT CONSIDERS THE FACIAL STICKERS PASSÉ. BOTH THESE TRENDS INVOLVE CREATING A MUCH DARKER SHADE OF SKIN THAN THAT OF ORDINARY GANGURO AND—AS BEFITS TRENDS TRYING TO MAKE AN EXISTING TREND EVEN MORE EXCLUSIVE—GIRLS TAKE OFFENSE AT BEING LABELED THE WRONG SUBCATEGORY.

❀

Chapter 5

Cultural Manias

BE IT A MOVEMENT, A TV SHOW, A BOOK, A BAND, OR A TOY, A TRUE CULTURAL MANIA GETS SO BIG THAT EVEN YOUR GRANDPARENTS HAVE HEARD OF IT. It's hard to see them coming, and even harder for the biggest skeptics to avoid knowing more about them than they ever wanted, unless they choose to move under a rock. Some objects of cultural mania, like the Beatles, will have an impact that lasts for generations. Others, like Tickle Me Elmo, briefly capture the public's imagination before becoming closet clutter. Still others, like disco, spark intense but pointless culture wars. Here are a few of the cultural manias that, for better or (too often) for worse, came to define their times.

Orchidelirium

Location: *Great Britain* | Time Frame: *1800s*

TODAY, GETTING THE PERFECT FLOWERS CAN BE AS SIMPLE AS PICKING UP THE PHONE AND CALLING YOUR LOCAL FLORIST. DURING ORCHIDELIRIUM, IT WAS MORE LIKELY TO INVOLVE DEATH-DEFYING ADVENTURE AND HUGE PILES OF CASH.

In 1818, packing peanuts were not yet invented and crumpled-up newspaper wasn't readily available in Brazil. So when English naturalist William John Swainson sent specimens back home from an expedition near Rio de Janeiro, he used wild orchids to pack what he considered more valuable cargo. When his package arrived, however, it was one of the orchids that had bloomed in transit that got the most attention.

The tropical flowers were an instant novelty in Victorian England, where the upper classes were just getting into the idea of glass-housed conservatories and ornate outdoor gardens. Orchids were perfect accessories for status-driven collectors. They grew in exotic, inaccessible locations, and roughly half of them didn't survive the boat trip back, making them that much more rare. The enormous number of

EVEN PERRY MASON GOT IN ON THE TREND. THE LATE ACTOR RAYMOND BURR WAS AN AVID ORCHID COLLECTOR, AND THE PRIVATE STASH HE CULTIVATED IN FIJI REMAINS ONE OF THE COUNTRY'S BIGGEST TOURIST ATTRACTIONS.

varieties made a diverse collection the mark of the truly wealthy and well connected. One particularly unusual orchid sold for £1,500 in 1890—which is about £97,000 in today's money. For a flower.

THE PINNACLE The craze got so crazy that collectors actually hired their own private explorers to seek

> ONE VIRGINIA COMPANY HAS A LONG-RUNNING TRADITION OF BREEDING HYBRID CATTLEYA ORCHID VARIETIES AND NAMING THEM FOR CELEBRITIES—INCLUDING A SERIES NAMED FOR AMERICA'S FIRST LADIES, AND OTHERS TAGGED AFTER MARGARET THATCHER, QUEEN ELIZABETH, AND MARTHA STEWART.

out more orchids, and the dangers orchid hunters faced sound like episodes of an adventure serial. A 1901 mission to the Philippines saw one crew member eaten by a tiger, another burned alive, and a few others mysteriously disappear in the jungle.

The damage the craze inflicted on human life was nothing compared to what it did to the natural world. Whole forests in the Andes were destroyed by orchid hunters searching for their prizes and successful hunters trashing the remnants so the competition couldn't get them. Scientists estimate that many thousands of orchid species disappeared from the wild during the peak of "Orchidelirium," which lasted until the end of the nineteenth century.

Orchid hunting can still be a dangerous undertaking today. In 2000, orchid hunters near the border of Panama and Colombia were captured by guerrillas and held for more than nine months. More than two hundred new orchid species continue to be discovered each year, and while the flowers are now protected in many places, smugglers still sell particularly rare ones for hundreds and even thousands of dollars.

Beatlemania

LOCATION: *Global* | TIME FRAME: *1960s*

LET'S JUST TAKE A MOMENT TO BE THANKFUL THAT THE FANS WENT CRAZY FOR A LEGITIMATELY GREAT BAND, BECAUSE FREDDIE-AND-THE-DREAMERS-MANIA WOULD'VE BEEN A REAL CULTURAL SNAFU.

It seems hard to believe now, but in 1962 the soon-to-be Fab Four—John Lennon, Paul McCartney, George Harrison, and new addition Ringo Starr—were still unknowns playing small clubs in Hamburg, Germany, and their hometown of Liverpool. That fall, though, they recorded two singles—"Love Me Do" and "Please Please Me"—that fared well on the UK charts, with the second a massive hit. Within a year, they went from playing for smallish crowds in smoky underground dives to performing for Queen Elizabeth, and being chased by mobs of screaming, hysterical fans.

> THE BAND WASN'T ALWAYS KNOWN AS THE BEATLES. OTHER NAMES INCLUDED THE BLACK JACKS, THE QUARRYMEN, AND JOHNNY AND THE MOONDOGS— BUT THE FINAL FOUR MEMBERS ONLY PLAYED TOGETHER AS THE BEATLES

WHY THE MANIA? It helped that girls quickly developed crushes on each of the boys (even Ringo), and guys rushed to copy them. Black suits like the matching ones the Beatles wore onstage started getting popular in the UK, as did the band's long hairstyles (and for those who couldn't grow them, the hot-selling Beatles wig). It also didn't hurt that all four Beatles were quick-witted masters of the one-liner, which got them plenty of interview time.

After becoming the biggest act in Britain by the end of 1963, the Beatles announced a trip to America and let the anticipation build. And build some more. By the time the band released "I Want to Hold Your Hand" across the pond that December, the average American teenager had heard a whole lot about them without ever actually hearing them—which didn't stop the single from becoming the all-time top seller in America.

DURING THE WEEK OF APRIL 4, 1964, THE BEATLES HELD THE TOP FIVE SPOTS ON THE U.S. *BILLBOARD* CHARTS (A FEAT THAT HASN'T BEEN REPEATED):

1. "CAN'T BUY ME LOVE"
2. "TWIST AND SHOUT"
3. "SHE LOVES YOU"
4. "I WANT TO HOLD YOUR HAND"
5. "PLEASE PLEASE ME"

Beatlemania in America went haywire on February 9, 1964, when an estimated 73 million people tuned in to watch the Beatles perform live on *The Ed Sullivan Show*. That would be more than one-third of the people in America at the time, and the rest soon learned all about what they missed because the Beatles were everywhere. The broadcast helped the band finally land a U.S. record deal, and delivered the kind of results usually reserved for a deal with the devil. By the time 1964 ended, the Beatles had nine of the year's

Top 40 songs on the American charts, including the two top spots. That's a record nobody's been able to touch forty years later, and will probably last until we're all living on Mars.

THE AFTERMATH By 1965, fan enthusiasm had become so intense that screaming crowds at the boys' concerts completely drowned out the band and soon encouraged the Beatles to permanently quit the road. From that point on, they impressively became a studio band only, without losing any of their popularity. Fans loved their more experimental music, and kept copying their more experimental lifestyle choices, from Day-Glo jackets to Transcendental Meditation to psychedelic drugs. While the band's 1970 breakup meant the Beatlemania craze eventually settled into more normal fandom, the Fab Four has still sold more albums than anybody else and all had successful solo careers. Even Ringo.

⇥❋⇤

THE BEATLES' LAST LIVE SHOW WAS ON AUGUST 29, 1966, IN SAN FRANCISCO'S CANDLESTICK PARK. THEY DIDN'T PLAY A SINGLE TRACK OF THEIR RECENTLY RELEASED *REVOLVER* ALBUM.

Disco

LOCATION: *Global* | TIME FRAME: *1970s*

THE DISCO EXPLOSION THAT DOMINATED THE NORTH AMERICAN MUSIC SCENE OF THE LATE 1970S COULD ALMOST PROVIDE THE BLUEPRINT FOR MANY A CULTURAL CRAZE: TAKE A LONG-STANDING, HIPPER-THAN-THOU SUBCULTURE, WATCH THE MAINSTREAM ADOPT IT, CO-OPT IT, THEN WAIT FOR THE INEVITABLE BACKLASH.

At the end of the 1960s, rock had taken over the music world, but the Woodstock generation's sound didn't lend itself well to dance parties. So a dance-crazed counterculture began to develop its own club scene—particularly in New York. As the scene grew, it soon created its own sound, featuring extended tracks, funk overtones, and steady dance-floor beats. Producers began cranking out new disco mixes specifically for club DJs, who played them for mostly gay, sexually liberated audiences in tightly packed clubs.

The club scene had cachet, and that made crossover success inevitable. By the middle of the 1970s, it was just as easy to hear extended disco mixes of hits like

> FEW TRENDS COULD INSPIRE SOMETHING LIKE 1979'S "DISCO DEMOLITION NIGHT," WHERE A CHICAGO DJ BLEW UP THOUSANDS OF DISCO RECORDS AT A WHITE SOX DOUBLEHEADER AT COMISKEY PARK. ONCE THE VINYL DETONATION BEGAN, MOST OF THE NINETY-THOUSAND-LARGE CROWD RUSHED THE FIELD, TRASHING THE GRASS AND FORCING THE WHITE SOX TO FORFEIT THE GAME IN THE PROCESS.

Donna Summer's "Love to Love You Baby" and Van McCoy's "The Hustle" on AM radio driving down Route 66 as it was in a sweaty underground club. Any doubt that the trend had gone mainstream was erased with the success of the 1975 John Travolta vehicle *Saturday Night Fever*, which became the iconic disco movie and came with a Bee Gees–heavy soundtrack that dominated the pop charts. The Bee Gees' conversion from pop to disco did wonders for their career, and other acts took notice. Before long, rock stars like David Bowie, Rod Stewart, and even the Rolling Stones were incorporating disco sounds into their repertoires, and new disco clubs like the notoriously

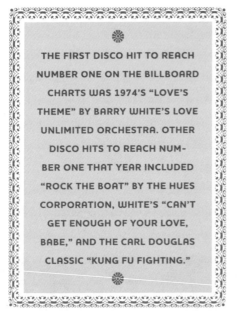

THE FIRST DISCO HIT TO REACH NUMBER ONE ON THE BILLBOARD CHARTS WAS 1974'S "LOVE'S THEME" BY BARRY WHITE'S LOVE UNLIMITED ORCHESTRA. OTHER DISCO HITS TO REACH NUMBER ONE THAT YEAR INCLUDED "ROCK THE BOAT" BY THE HUES CORPORATION, WHITE'S "CAN'T GET ENOUGH OF YOUR LOVE, BABE," AND THE CARL DOUGLAS CLASSIC "KUNG FU FIGHTING."

decadent Studio 54 became trendy destinations for celebrities.

THE PINNACLE The popularity of what had started as a counterculture to the counterculture wound up prompting a massive counterattack from the rock world. "Disco Sucks" became a T-shirt slogan staple, and the burgeoning punk movement defined itself in part as a reaction against the dance craze. Still, disco has refused to die. Need proof? Go to any wedding in America, and there's a good chance you'll see people dancing to the Village People's "YMCA" without irony. Or pay close attention to the samples on your favorite hip-hop tracks. It's no longer the scene it once was, but disco is (ahem) stayin' alive.

Michael Jackson's *Thriller*

LOCATION: *Global* | TIME FRAME: *1982–1983*

BEFORE ANYONE HAD ITUNES OR DOWNLOADED MUSIC ILLEGALLY, IT WAS STILL POSSIBLE TO MAKE AN ALBUM THAT EVERYBODY BOUGHT. AND JUST ABOUT EVERYBODY BOUGHT MICHAEL JACKSON'S 1982 ALBUM, *THRILLER*.

Between his Motown days with the Jackson 5 and his impressive solo career (critics and audiences absolutely loved 1979's *Off the Wall*), Jackson was already a big star when he and producer Quincy Jones started working on *Thriller*. But Jackson wanted more, telling his manager he wanted *Thriller* to make him "the biggest star in show business." Did it ever.

Jackson reportedly worked on more than three hundred potential album tracks before settling on the final nine. He enlisted the help of superstar friends, cowriting "The Girl Is Mine" with Paul McCartney and hiring Eddie Van Halen to play guitar on "Beat It." Jones and Jackson remixed each of the final tracks repeatedly, spending at least a week on each one.

> "THRILLER" ALMOST WASN'T "THRILLER." AN EARLY VERSION OF THE SONG WAS CALLED "STARLIGHT," WITH A CHORUS OF "STARLIGHT! STARLIGHT SUN." WHICH IS PROOF THAT SECOND DRAFTS CAN BE A GOOD IDEA.

WHY THE MANIA? To say all that work paid off would define understatement, as no record ever set more records. *Thriller* became the first album in history to have seven top-ten singles—more impressive considering only seven of the nine tracks were even released as singles. *Thriller* won a record eight Grammys. It took less than a year to become the best-selling album of all time (both in the United States and abroad), and still holds that record more than two decades later.

> AN OSCAR NOMINATION PROVED THE RARE ACCOLADE *THRILLER* FAILED TO EARN. THE VIDEO PLAYED IN A LOS ANGELES–AREA THEATER FOR A WEEK IN 1983 (BEFORE SCREENINGS OF DISNEY'S *FANTASIA*) WITH THE GOAL OF MAKING IT ELIGIBLE FOR AN ACADEMY AWARD. VOTERS DIDN'T APPRECIATE THE EFFORT.

Music video was another area where *Thriller* made an immediate impact. There was so much demand for Michael that "Billie Jean" became the first video by a black artist to air on the young MTV network, and "Beat It" soon followed. For the album's title track, Jackson recorded a fourteen-minute video that was more like a short film, with a memorable vocal performance by horror legend Vincent Price. Jackson cowrote the script with *Animal House* and *The Blues Brothers* director John Landis, who filmed the acclaimed short. It was such a huge hit that MTV played it twice an hour, making it America's most popular rerun. Jackson's dancing and choreography might have been as influential as the music itself, with the "Moonwalk" and "Thriller" dances becoming staples on dance floors around the world.

It would have been hard to top the success of *Thriller*, though Jackson continued to release hit albums and singles. A twenty-fifth-anniversary edition returned *Thriller* to the charts, and it peaked again when its creator died suddenly at age fifty in 2009.

M*A*S*H Final Episode

LOCATION: *United States* | TIME FRAME: *1983*

TALK ABOUT GOING OUT ON TOP. ON MONDAY NIGHT, FEBRUARY 28, 1983, NEARLY 106 MILLION AMERICANS—ROUGHLY 77 PERCENT OF *ALL* TELEVISION WATCHERS—SWITCHED ON CBS FOR THE FINAL EPISODE OF *M*A*S*H*. THAT MADE "GOODBYE, FAREWELL AND AMEN," THE SHOW'S 251ST AND LAST INSTALLMENT, THE HIGHEST-RATED SHOW IN HISTORY.

In its eleven years on the air, *M*A*S*H* had survived changes that would have killed a lesser series. When it debuted in 1972, it already had the burden of living up to Robert Altman's critically acclaimed 1970 film while having different actors play many of the characters (Gary Burghoff, though, played Radar in both versions). Low viewing figures almost led CBS to cancel the show during its first season. The show matured during its run, adding more dramatic situations to what had started as a sitcom (though it always kept its sense of humor) and driving home its antiwar message at a time when Vietnam was still a very

---

TO GET A SENSE OF HOW IMPRESSIVE THE FINALE'S 105.9 MILLION VIEWERS WERE, CONSIDER THE NUMBERS FOR THE NEXT MOST-WATCHED FINALES: *CHEERS* (80.4 MILLION), *SEINFELD* (76.3 MILLION), AND *FRIENDS* (52.5 MILLION).

---

immediate concern. It went on to become a huge hit, lasting eight years longer than the Korean conflict during which it was set.

When it came time to wish its flagship show good-bye and farewell, CBS turned the broadcast into an event. Rather than a normal half-hour episode, the finale ran two and a half hours. Advertisers who wanted their commercials to run during the much-hyped episode had to pay more than they did for that year's Super Bowl. The network spent weeks promoting the finale, and the producers put together an all-star team of collaborators to write it. One of the show's more dramatic episodes, it closed with the doctors and nurses of the 4077th heading their separate ways after the fighting ended with a cease-fire, wrapping up each character's story line. Unless you count the short-lived spin-off *AfterMASH*—and you really shouldn't—the last shots of Alan Alda looking down from a helicopter at the word "good-bye" (spelled out below in stones) gave fans a fitting farewell to all their favorite characters.

✺

BEFORE THE *M*A*S*H* FINALE, THE MOST-WATCHED SHOW IN HISTORY WAS THE ANSWER TO THE "WHO SHOT J.R.?" CLIFFHANGER ON *DALLAS*. (SPOILER ALERT: IT WASN'T YOUR NEIGHBOR WITH THE "I SHOT J.R." T-SHIRT.)

✺

THE AFTERMATH No program ever drew more viewers than the *M*A*S*H* finale until the 2010 Super Bowl, which, to get technical, had a far lower audience share but a slightly larger total audience, which is kind of cheating. Plenty of popular shows have since turned their finales into monster hits, but none quite so successfully as Alan Alda and company. With the prevalence of cable, television on demand, and streaming video, it seems pretty unlikely that anything will ever get such a huge chunk of the population to all watch at the same time ever again.

WrestleMania

LOCATION: *United States* | TIME FRAME: *1985*

SURE, THE WRESTLING IN VINCE MCMAHON'S WORLD WRESTLING ENTERTAINMENT MAY BE FAKE, BUT THE MAN'S GOT A VERY REAL TALENT WHEN IT COMES TO MARKETING.

When McMahon took over his father's thirty-year-old wrestling business in 1982, pro wrestling was mostly a regional thing with various federations staking out different territories. Wisely sensing an opportunity, McMahon began syndicating the then–World Wrestling Federation's matches on national television. So he became the first wrestling promoter with a nationwide product, which made it easier for him to take his show on the road in arenas around the country, and to become one of the first people to successfully market sports videos in the early days of the VCR. All that money and exposure helped McMahon wrestle the best talent away from his competitors, and he soon signed virtually all the sport's major stars, including Hulk Hogan, Andre the Giant, and future Minnesota governor Jesse "The Body" Ventura.

Just in case anyone even thought of challenging his WWF's new title as king of the ring, McMahon had

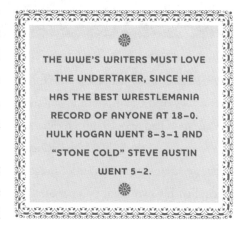

THE WWE'S WRITERS MUST LOVE THE UNDERTAKER, SINCE HE HAS THE BEST WRESTLEMANIA RECORD OF ANYONE AT 18–0. HULK HOGAN WENT 8–3–1 AND "STONE COLD" STEVE AUSTIN WENT 5–2.

another ambitious brainstorm. Just three years into his ownership, WWF held the first WrestleMania in 1985. The March 31 event at Madison Square Garden, heavily promoted on WWF broadcasts, was shown live nationwide on pay-per-view and included a full slate of matches featuring the biggest names among McMahon's wrestlers. Special guest stars included singer Cyndi Lauper and actor Mr. T.

THE PINNACLE More than a million fans reportedly tuned in to the event, setting a record for pay-per-view programming. WrestleMania only grew from there, becoming an annual centerpiece of the WWF (now the WWE) "season." By year three, more than ninety thousand fans—then a record for any indoor event—packed the Detroit–area Silverdome to see the now-famous finale between Hogan and Andre the Giant.

> MCMAHON WASN'T CONTENT TO JUST OWN THE WWE. HE HIRED HIMSELF AS AN ANNOUNCER, LATER MADE HIS ADULT KIDS INTO CHARACTERS ON THE SHOW, AND (AFTER A LOT OF MUSCLING UP) REGULARLY WRESTLED AGAINST HIS STARS. HIS DAUGHTER EVEN MARRIED WRESTLER TRIPLE H IN REAL LIFE *AND* ON TV.

WrestleMania clearly established the WWF as the muscle in the wrestling world. It took a brief hit in the early 1990s, when a series of steroid and sexual harassment allegations forced McMahon to cut performers' salaries and let rival World Championship Wrestling get an edge. By the middle of the decade, McMahon had retooled his product to make it edgier, replacing the family-friendly "good guys" of the 1980s with antiheroes who drank and gave the finger. Wrestling fans apparently wanted to root for the bad guys. By decade's end, McMahon had acquired his two main competitors, launched two highly rated weekly wrestling shows, and created his own movie studio and record label to promote his stars.

The Atkins Diet

LOCATION: *United States* | TIME FRAME: *2003–2004*

CONVINCE AMERICANS THAT THEY CAN LOSE WEIGHT BY STUFFING THEIR FACES WITH BACON, ICE CREAM, AND GREASY FAST-FOOD BURGERS—PROVIDED THEY LEAVE OFF THE BUN—AND YOU HAVE A RECIPE FOR THE ULTIMATE FAD DIET.

In a country with one of the world's highest obesity rates, fad diets are nothing new. After all, grapefruit, oat bran, cabbage, and meal-replacement shakes all had their day. From 2003 to 2004, however, the low-carbohydrate diet pitched by Dr. Robert Atkins got bigger than Americans' waistlines. First published in his 1972 book, *Dr. Atkins' Diet Revolution: The High Calorie Way to Stay Thin Forever*—and how's *that* for a sales pitch—Atkins claimed his diet led to weight loss because limiting carbohydrates would alter the body's metabolism and force it to burn stored body fat. He advocated eliminating carbohydrate-heavy foods, like potatoes and bread, replacing them with more meat, dairy, and fish.

Acting more like a salesman than a trained cardiologist, Atkins published (and republished) a series of books touting his diet and founded a company called Atkins

> DR. ATKINS PUBLISHED MORE THAN A DOZEN BOOKS ABOUT HIS CONTROVERSIAL DIET. THE MOST POPULAR, *DR. ATKINS' NEW DIET REVOLUTION*, SPENT SIX YEARS ON THE *NEW YORK TIMES* BESTSELLER LIST AND (BETWEEN SEVERAL EDITIONS) SOLD ABOUT 15 MILLION COPIES.

Nutritionals to sell low-carb foods. It took a while, but his plan came to fruition by 2003, when roughly 12 percent of Americans reported trying to cut carbs

THE ATKINS CRAZE EVEN INSPIRED SEVERAL LOW-CARB CRUISES, WHERE DIETERS COULD TRAVEL THE CARIBBEAN TOGETHER WHILE BOYCOTTING BREAD AND LISTENING TO LECTURES BY PRO-ATKINS SPEAKERS.

and the Atkins diet helped drive beef, pork, and eggs to their highest sales figures in years. Companies rushed to capitalize on the trend, with Burger King selling bun-less burgers, Subway introducing a low-carb bacon sub, and Michelob flogging low-carb beer.

THE AFTERMATH Like a crash dieter seeing the pounds come right back, the popularity of the Atkins diet soon collapsed. Atkins died in 2003 from head injuries he suffered when he slipped on ice, and reports of his weighing 258 pounds at the time certainly didn't help promote his diet. (Nor did the revelation of a medical examiner's report noting he suffered from hypertension and congestive heart failure.) By late 2004, sales of Atkins Nutritionals products had fallen sharply, and the company filed for Chapter 11 bankruptcy in July 2005.

The demise of the low-carb trend also had a lot to do with the public learning more about its risks. It's a rare diet that the American Medical Association calls "the most dangerous" diet fad in fifty years, or that unites the American Dietetic Association, American Heart Association, and American Cancer Society in vehement opposition. Atkins's weight-loss claims were never scientifically proven, but the diet *was* proven to greatly increase the risks of gout, hypertension, high cholesterol, heart disease—and any number of ailments far more dangerous than a few extra pounds.

Cabbage Patch Kids

LOCATION: *North America* | TIME FRAME: *1983*

THEY HAD SOFT BODIES, SURPRISINGLY HARD HEADS, AND BECAME 1980S ICONS. NO, NOT YUPPIES. CABBAGE PATCH KIDS.

The dolls were the brainchild of Xavier Roberts, a young craftsman from Cleveland, Georgia, who started making them while working his way through school. He sold his first dolls—called "Little People"—at craft shows around the Southeast, and had the idea of giving each doll a unique "birth certificate," making slight changes to each doll to ensure no two were identical, and calling his transactions "adoptions" rather than sales.

His unusual methods worked. The dolls inspired articles in publications like *Newsweek* and the *Wall Street Journal*. Demand far outpaced supply almost immediately,

> IN 1978, ROBERTS BOUGHT AN OUT-OF-USE MEDICAL FACILITY IN HIS HOMETOWN, RENAMING IT BABYLAND GENERAL HOSPITAL. HE RENOVATED IT INTO A DOLL "HOSPITAL" (AKA PRODUCTION FACILITY) WITH A BIRTHING SECTION, A NURSERY SECTION, AND AN ADOPTION CENTER WHERE WOULD-BE "PARENTS" COULD CHOOSE A KID. THE COST OF BUYING THE DOLLS WAS NEVER A "PRICE," BUT ALWAYS AN "ADOPTION FEE."

so Roberts sold mass production rights for his dolls to Coleco in 1982. Coleco made the heads vinyl rather than cloth and changed the name to Cabbage Patch Kids, but kept the birth certificate and individuality. With their puffy cheeks, homely faces, belly buttons, and preselected names, the Cabbage Patch Kids had a distinct look that stood out from the competition.

THE PINNACLE In their first year, nearly 3 million Cabbage Patch Kids were "adopted," making them the most successful new doll in history. Befitting their status as the "it" toys of 1983, Cabbage Patch Kids also inspired their share of shopping insanity, with parents getting in fights over the in-demand dolls. By 1985, Coleco was selling $600 million worth of Cabbage Patch dolls, accessories, and spin-off products.

TALK ABOUT A SUCCESSFUL LAUNCH: IN 1985, NASA SENT A CABBAGE PATCH KID INTO OUTER SPACE ABOARD A SHUTTLE MISSION.

The company kept releasing new varieties, including "Koosas"—cats and dogs in the Cabbage Patch style—and "Preemies," introducing children to the notion of risky premature birth, but that couldn't stop the inevitable slowdown. In 1988, just a few years after the dolls conquered the world, Coleco was a reported $300 million in debt and had to file for bankruptcy, forcing it to sell the Cabbage Patch brand. Over time, Hasbro, Mattel, and Toys "R" Us took turns producing the dolls—with a company called Play Along currently doing the honors—but none has ever managed to recapture the peak of their popularity.

Tickle Me Elmo

LOCATION: *North America* | TIME FRAME: *1996*

SESAME STREET ALWAYS TAUGHT CHILDREN THE VALUE OF SHARING, BUT THEIR PARENTS TURNED DECIDEDLY CUTTHROAT WHEN IT CAME TO BUYING A TOY VERSION OF THE SHOW'S FURRY RED MONSTER.

Around the holiday season in 1996, shoppers went berserk for Tickle Me Elmo. Sure, it was a cute toy—basically a plush version of the popular *Sesame Street* character that giggled or said, "That tickles," when children pushed certain spots—but parents treated it like the Holy Grail. Blame it on savvy marketing or a herd mentality, but the $30 doll became the must-have toy that year and inspired people to go to crazy lengths to get one before Christmas morning.

It all started when influential TV host Rosie O'Donnell gave away a promotional batch of the Tyco-made dolls in October 1996, but no one was prepared for what happened the day after Thanksgiving. On the busiest

---

⊰✳⊱

HOW BAD DID THE ELMO CRAZE GET IN 1996? ONE COMMUNITY SELLING ELMOS FOR CHARITY HAD TO LOCK THEM IN A PRISON CELL TO THWART WOULD-BE THIEVES. CARTIER PLACED ONE IN A STORE WINDOW, MAKING IT THE GIFT-WITH-PURCHASE ON A MILLION-DOLLAR NECKLACE.

---

shopping day of the year, it took only a couple of hours for Tickle Me Elmo to sell out of stores throughout the country. Tyco didn't expect it to be *that* popular, and struggled to keep Elmo in stock. The limited availability made the toy even more desirable. And with online auction sites like eBay just starting to get big, shoppers who grabbed a few extra dolls were able to sell them at several times their face value (the highest reported sale was around $1,500). By the time the holiday rush was over, Tyco was tickled to find it had sold more than a million Elmos, and it went on to sell more than five million by the end of 1997.

> A WAL-MART CLERK SUFFERED BROKEN BONES AND A CONCUSSION WHEN A CROWD OF SHOPPERS SAW HIM HOLDING SOME DOLLS AND LITERALLY RAN HIM OVER IN THEIR EXCITEMENT.

THE AFTERMATH For whatever reason, shoppers were calmer when it came to subsequent *Sesame Street* dolls. Tickle Me versions of Cookie Monster, Ernie, Big Bird, and other characters were also introduced and sold well, but didn't inspire anything near the insane popularity that Elmo had. Nor did future Elmos, one released each year, with varieties like Let's Pretend Elmo and Chicken Dance Elmo. The closest was the T.M.X. Elmo, a tenth-anniversary Tickle Me Elmo with additional behaviors released in 2006. That one also became the most popular holiday toy of its year, but didn't come close to the 1996 hysteria.

Harry Potter

LOCATION: *Global* | TIME FRAME: *1997–2007*

WITH HER HARRY POTTER SERIES, BRITISH AUTHOR J. K. ROWLING PULLED OFF A FEAT OF MAGIC THAT WOULD IMPRESS ANY OF HER WIZARD CHARACTERS. SHE GOT KIDS EXCITED ABOUT READING SEVEN-HUNDRED-PAGE BOOKS.

For those who've been living under a rock for the past decade, Rowling's book series concerns Harry Potter (obviously), an orphan who on his eleventh birthday learns not only that he is a wizard, but that the evil wizard Voldemort murdered his parents and tried to murder him. Harry enrolls at Hogwart's, a boarding school for young wizards, where he meets the friends, teachers, and rivals who populate the whole series. Rowling's genius was in her ability to combine several popular genres—mixing fantasy, mystery, and drama—and draw in fans of each. Her books also grew with her readers, both in length (the first book is 300 pages in the United States; the longest is 870 pages) and in style, with each volume getting darker in tone and more complex in plotting.

WORRIED THAT USING HER REAL FIRST NAME (JOANNE, BY THE WAY) WOULD MAKE YOUNG BOYS SEE THE NOVEL AS "FOR GIRLS," HER PUBLISHER INSISTED ON CREDITING ROWLING BY HER GENDER-NEUTRAL INITIALS.

THE FINAL BOOK IN THE SERIES, *HARRY POTTER AND THE HALF-BLOOD PRINCE*, SOLD 11 MILLION COPIES IN ITS FIRST TWENTY-FOUR HOURS.

POTTER-MANIA Of course, none of that would have mattered if audiences didn't love the books, which they did right away. The first, *Harry Potter and the Philosopher's Stone*, was such a hit when it was published in 1997 in the UK that Rowling received six figures for the American publication in 1998.

The series drew more fans with each book, and the anticipation for a new Potter volume became a craze in itself. Rowling's announcements of release dates were major news items, and the series set all kinds of records for preorders and first-day sales, with bookstores capitalizing by holding midnight release parties for young fans who arrived in costumes of cloaks, hats, and glasses. By 2008, Rowling had sold more than 400 million Harry Potter books in sixty-seven different languages—numbers that top just about everything but the Bible.

Anything that popular was going to have a huge cultural impact. Potter's success prompted the *New York Times* to launch a separate best-seller list for children's literature in 2000. All the film adaptations rank among the twenty-five highest-grossing movies of all time worldwide, and the Universal Orlando theme park even opened a Wizarding World of Harry Potter in 2010.

After the Potter series finished, children's publishing in general (and Rowling's publisher, Scholastic, in particular) took a financial nosedive. As for Rowling, she released a short book of wizard tales referenced in a Potter book, then took a deserved break from writing.

Twilight Series

LOCATION: *Global* | TIME FRAME: *2005-2010*

TO A WHOLE GENERATION OF TEEN GIRLS, VAMPIRES ARE NOW NO LONGER CREEPY, BLOODSUCKING CREATURES OF THE NIGHT BUT *TIGER BEAT* TYPES WHO CAN WALK AROUND IN SUNLIGHT WITH NO ILL EFFECTS—ALL THE BETTER TO GLEAM DOWN ON THEIR PERFECT BODIES.

For that you can blame–or thank, if you're into it–Stephenie Meyer and her wildly successful Twilight series. By, um, defanging vampire mythology and mixing it with the style of a romance novel, she became one of the most financially successful new authors of the twenty-first century and the center of a multimillion-dollar empire Bram Stoker could never have envisioned.

The four-part book series is the story of Bella Swan, a teenage girl who comes to Forks, Washington, to live with her dad. At school, she meets and falls for Edward Cullen, who happens to be a vampire and can conveniently attend school *during the day*. The books—*Twilight, New Moon, Eclipse*, and *Breaking Dawn*—focus on the couple's romance and the obstacles they have to overcome—like werewolves, revenge-seeking vampires, and the edicts of a coven of vampire elders. Critical reaction

> "TWILIGHT" MANIA EVEN CHANGED WHAT PEOPLE CALL THEIR KIDS, AS IT'S CREDITED WITH HELPING NAMES LIKE BELLA, EDWARD, AND JACOB RISE IN POPULARITY.

to the books was decidedly mixed, but Meyer's decision to write in Bella's first-person voice and leave her narrator lightly developed allowed teen girls—and a disturbing number of older women—to project themselves into the character.

THE REAL TOWN OF FORKS HAS SEEN A HUGE SPIKE IN TOURISM, AND CAPITALIZED WITH "TWILIGHT" TOURS AND SHOPS SELLING "TWILIGHT"-THEMED MERCHANDISE.

WHY THE MANIA? Despite her lack of literary credentials, publishers knew Meyer was onto something with her first manuscript, which netted her a three-book deal worth an impressive $750,000. And her sales proved them right. Starting with the 2005 release of *Twilight*, all four books were bestsellers—with a combined total of more than 100 million copies so far—and in 2008, Meyer became the first author to hold the top four spots on *USA Today*'s best-seller list at the same time. In June 2010, after announcing an end to the Twilight series, she published a companion novella called *The Short Second Life of Bree Tanner*, which fans could read for free (but not download) at the author's Web site.

Producers of the Twilight films struck while the phenomenon was still hot, releasing a Twilight installment annually starting in November 2008, with the first two volumes easily earning nine figures each and turning little-known actors Robert Pattinson and Taylor Lautner into teen heartthrobs. Like the walking undead at its heart, the Twilight craze refused to die.

Chapter 6

Technological Trends and Fears

STARTING WITH THE INDUSTRIAL REVOLUTION, FEW THINGS HAVE CONSISTENTLY CHANGED THE WORLD MORE THAN TECHNOLOGY. All those technological advances, however, have both pluses and minuses. Sure, they can make your job easier, but they can also eliminate the need for your job altogether. They can give one company or country a great advantage . . . at least until the competition comes up with something better. And, if you're an early adopter, the gadgets almost always drop in price right after you buy them. From weaving machines to Russian satellites to computer viruses, the one thing technology always seems to inspire is rampant technophobia.

The Luddites

LOCATION: *Great Britain* | TIME FRAME: *1812*

IT'S A SHAME THAT THE WORD "LUDDITE" HAS BECOME A CATCHALL TERM FOR TECHNOPHOBES. AFTER ALL, THE LUDDITE MOVEMENT HAD A VERY SPECIFIC AND REALLY GOOD REASON FOR HATING TECHNOLOGY. AND THE LUDDITES DIDN'T JUST WHINGE; THEY DID SOMETHING ABOUT IT.

When the Luddite movement started in 1812, weavers in England had a good thing going. As they had done for centuries, they were able to make a respectable living as artisans, working from home rather than in dangerous factories. Because their high-quality textiles were handmade and prices were well established, they could sell their wares for good money throughout the realm and even overseas.

The industrial revolution threatened that very way of life with the invention of the stocking frame. A mechanical knitting device, it eliminated the need for skilled craftsmen by making weaving faster and more uniform, letting the machine do most of the work. The machines were too expensive for individuals to buy, but

> THE LUDDITES TOOK THEIR NAME IN HONOR OF NED LUDD, A YOUNG WEAVER WHO BROKE A PAIR OF STOCKING FRAMES IN LEICESTERSHIRE IN 1779. ACCOUNTS DIFFER AS TO WHETHER LUDD BROKE THE MACHINES OUT OF ANGER OR CLUMSINESS—AND EVEN WHETHER HE ACTUALLY EXISTED.

THE LATEST CRAZE

130

large cotton or wool mills could easily afford them, and they had the capacity to produce lots and lots of merchandise. Which, in turn, meant lower prices for woven goods—and also meant artisan weavers could say good-bye to their work-from-home jobs and decent salaries.

THE PINNACLE Unwilling to go quietly, some of those weavers formed a guerrilla group to destroy factory machines. Part John Henry, part Robin Hood, the Luddites would often camp out near industrial towns before launching their attacks. Fittingly starting in Nottingham, the Luddites became such a threat that the English gov-

THE MOVEMENT ALSO MADE ITS MARK ON LITERATURE. CHARLOTTE BRONTË SET HER CLASSIC NOVEL *SHIRLEY* DURING THE LUDDITE UPRISINGS, WHILE WRITERS LIKE JONATHAN SWIFT AND RALPH WALDO EMERSON HAVE SOMETIMES BEEN LABELED "NEO-LUDDITES" FOR THEIR VIEWS ON TECHNOLOGY.

ernment actually passed a Frame Breaking Act that made industrial sabotage a death-penalty crime, and seventeen Luddites were executed after one 1813 trial. Several battles pitted the English military against hundreds of armed Luddites, with captured guerrillas executed or sent to penal colonies in Australia.

While most Luddite campaigns focused on sabotage, one infamous attack involved the assassination of a mill owner, and the harsh crackdown afterward began to kill the movement as even some supporters thought things had gone too far. Occasional Luddite-like uprisings cropped up in various industries over the next few decades, but the pace of technological advancement ultimately proved a far more effective enemy to the movement than either the army or the police.

Sputnik

ROM TODAY'S PERSPECTIVE, IT'S EASY TO LOOK BACK AT THE OCTOBER 4, 1957, LAUNCH OF THE SOVIET SATELLITE *SPUTNIK* AS THE BEGINNING OF AN AMAZING SPACE AGE THAT BROUGHT THE WORLD UNTOLD WONDERS OF NEW TECHNOLOGY AND OPENED OUR IMAGINATIONS TO THE IDEA OF A MAN ON THE MOON. AS OPPOSED TO A REASON TO RUN IN TERROR.

At the time, though, the United States and USSR had already gone from joining forces to defeat Hitler to competing with each other to build the biggest nuclear arsenal and pointing said arsenals at one another. Living in a world where kids practiced the duck-and-cover at school, Americans saw the beach ball–size, orbiting satellite as the first strike in a battle to control outer space. The anxiety *Sputnik* sparked came from a scarier concern: If Russia could launch a satellite into outer space so quickly, without the United States having any idea beforehand, who was to say it couldn't do the same with a nuclear

---

⊰※⊱

THE RUSSIANS PICKED UP ANOTHER BIG VICTORY IN THE SPACE RACE
IN APRIL 1961, WHEN COSMONAUT YURI GAGARIN BECAME THE FIRST MAN
TO REACH OUTER SPACE. THE FOLLOWING MONTH, ALAN B. SHEPARD, JR.
TOOK THE TITLE OF FIRST AMERICAN TO DO IT.

---

missile? Before *Sputnik* launched, most Americans had never imagined the concept of a man-made satellite orbiting the earth; by the day after the launch, they were urging their government to get one up as soon as humanly possible.

THE AFTERMATH Of course, America was already working on space technology before *Sputnik*, but seeing the USSR so far ahead technologically couldn't help but spark the Eisenhower administration into ramping up the budget for space exploration (and the Democratic Congress into establishing the new agency we know as NASA). The United States tried to launch a satellite named *Vanguard* on December 6, but it crumbled embarrassingly upon launch. It wasn't until *Explorer 1* in January 1958 that the country even managed to get a satellite into orbit—by which point the

AN UNFORTUNATE DOG NAMED LAIKA WAS THE FIRST PASSENGER TO GO INTO OUTER SPACE (AND THE FIRST LEFT TO DIE IN SPACE) A MONTH LATER IN THE SECOND OF MANY *SPUTNIK* MISSIONS. AT LEAST SHE HAS BEEN POSTHUMOUSLY HONORED, WITH A STATUE IN MOSCOW AND A POSTAGE STAMP. THE USSR SENT THIRTEEN DOGS INTO SPACE BETWEEN 1957 AND 1961, WITH EIGHT RETURNING ALIVE.

Russians had already sent up their second *Sputnik*. Still, John F. Kennedy made the space race a major goal of his administration, and the United States soon caught up. America pulled ahead for good once Neil Armstrong took his giant step on the moon for mankind, just twelve years after the USSR's little beeping ball started the whole ordeal.

Betamax vs. VHS

LOCATION: *Global* | TIME FRAME: *1970s–1980s*

SOME PRODUCT WARS GO ON FOREVER, LIKE COKE VERSUS PEPSI OR McDONALD'S VERSUS BURGER KING. OTHERS ARE A SHORT SKIRMISH WITH A CLEAR VICTOR, MORE FALKLANDS WAR THAN HUNDRED YEARS' WAR. THE EPIC CLASH OF VHS AND BE-TAMAX WAS ONE OF THE LATTER.

The VCR actually debuted in 1972, but Sony's introduction of Betamax in 1975 marked the first version of the technology that regular people actually bought, despite the high price tag. For the first time, people could watch their favorite show without having to design their entire night around it. Unfortunately for Sony, Betamax got a competitor when JVC released its VHS format two years later, and the newcomer took a big lead quickly.

Time was on the side of the VHS, in the sense that it had a much longer recording time. When Betamax first appeared, it could only record sixty minutes on a tape, which made it useful for recording one show while watching another but way too short for consumers who wanted

> ❀
>
> TOSHIBA AND SANYO, BOTH BETAMAX SUPPORTERS WHO PRODUCED MACHINES COMPATIBLE WITH THE FORMAT, GOT BURNED AGAIN IN THE 2000S, WHEN THEY SUPPORTED THE HD DVD IN A LOSING FORMAT WAR AGAINST BLU-RAY DISC FOR THE HIGH-DEFINITION DISC MARKET. MAYBE A THIRD TIME WILL BE THE CHARM.
>
> ❀

to go out on Friday and still see the movie of the week. It wasn't long before movie studios wanted to hawk priced-to-own movies, and VHS was already able to handle the workload with 120- and 180-minute tapes. By the time Betamax caught up, VHS was firmly established as the go-to videotape for home video, and dominated the video stores opening in every town. By 1980, VHS had about 70 percent of the market, and it never gave up its role as the alpha.

THE AFTERMATH Some techies will still argue that Betamax was the better format, but the people had clearly spoken. In January 1988, Sony finally caved by starting to make its own VHS machines and phasing out the Betamax. By 1998, the machines were only being produced for the Japanese market, and even that ceased by the end of 2002, leaving one of Sony's breakthrough products little more than a collector's item. On the schadenfreude front, the rise of DVD made VHS's victory relatively short-lived, and JVC made its last VHS machine in 2007.

AMONG THE FIRST MOVIES RELEASED ON HOME VIDEO IN AMERICA WERE *PATTON*, *M*A*S*H*, AND *THE SOUND OF MUSIC*. THEY COST BETWEEN FIFTY AND SEVENTY DOLLARS A POP. THE LAST U.S. VHS RELEASE WAS *A HISTORY OF VIOLENCE* IN 2006.

Computer Viruses

IN 1971, A NUMBER OF COMPUTER SCREENS SUDDENLY DISPLAYED THE CRYPTIC MESSAGE "I'M THE CREEPER, CATCH ME IF YOU CAN!" WITH THAT, AMERICA WAS FORMALLY INTRODUCED TO THE COMPUTER VIRUS.

Loosely defined as software programs that replicate themselves and damage computer files, computer viruses were a minor nuisance early in their history. After all, relatively few computers were online in those days, meaning a virus had to spread through discs or other removable devices. Plus, most early viruses were contained in the labs where they started, and often consisted of techies showing off their coding skills to one another with allegedly clever programs.

Elk Cloner, the first known virus to spread to the general public, debuted in 1982. To get a sense of how long ago that was, consider that it infected Apple II computers, and only when the machine booted—remember booting?—from an infected floppy. More practical joke than computer killer, the virus just made infected machines show a silly poem touting it as "the program with a personality." (Not surprisingly, it was designed by a fifteen-year-old boy.) The following year, a doctoral candidate at USC coined the term "computer virus" to describe these programs, and the name proved

NEW VIRUSES AND MALWARE ARE CONSTANT PAINS FOR
COMPUTER USERS. AMONG THE ALL-TIME TOP OFFENDERS:

GREAT WORM. THIS 1988 WORM DID MASSIVE DAMAGE,
KNOCKING OUT ALL GOVERNMENT AND COMMERCIAL
INTERNET ACTIVITY FOR WEEKS.

MELISSA. IN 1999, IT INFECTED MICROSOFT OFFICE FILES,
AND SPREAD BY SENDING ITSELF TO THE FIRST FIFTY
CONTACTS IN EACH USER'S OUTLOOK ADDRESS BOOK.

I LOVE YOU. USERS HATED THIS 2000 BUG, WHICH INFECTED
MILLIONS OF COMPUTERS. THE FILIPINO STUDENT WHO
CREATED IT GOT OFF SCOT-FREE BECAUSE THE PHILIPPINES HAD
NO LAW AGAINST SENDING VIRUSES.

ANNA KOURNIKOVA. A WORM LAUNCHED IN 2001, IT PROMISED
PHOTOS OF THE RUSSIAN TENNIS STARLET, BUT CLICKING ON
IT GAVE THE USER MALWARE INSTEAD.

NIMDA. JUST DAYS AFTER THE SEPTEMBER 11 ATTACKS,
THIS OPPORTUNISTIC VIRUS HIT THOUSANDS OF COMPUTERS
WHILE THEIR ADMINISTRATORS WERE DISTRACTED.

communicable. Along with viruses, users also had to contend with worms (programs that copy themselves and "worm" their way through entire networks), Trojan horses (which sneak into your system, wait awhile, and then attack), and other malware (malicious software) that technically aren't true viruses—though that distinction doesn't mean much to you when they're wiping out your term paper.

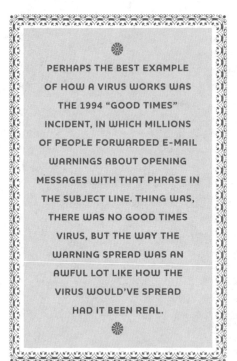

PERHAPS THE BEST EXAMPLE OF HOW A VIRUS WORKS WAS THE 1994 "GOOD TIMES" INCIDENT, IN WHICH MILLIONS OF PEOPLE FORWARDED E-MAIL WARNINGS ABOUT OPENING MESSAGES WITH THAT PHRASE IN THE SUBJECT LINE. THING WAS, THERE WAS NO GOOD TIMES VIRUS, BUT THE WAY THE WARNING SPREAD WAS AN AWFUL LOT LIKE HOW THE VIRUS WOULD'VE SPREAD HAD IT BEEN REAL.

THE PINNACLE Viruses really started to enter "the wild" in the late 1980s and early 1990s, as more and more computer users got connected. Initially, this meant that bulletin boards where users swapped software became favorite targets for viruses and hackers. At first software companies weren't too concerned about helping, considering most of the swapped software was bootlegged or copied illegally. As more people started using the Internet and found their computers exposed to viruses, companies saw that there was a market for protection from these programs. The first version of Norton AntiVirus was released in 1991, and dozens of antivirus programs followed. Ever since, hackers have created new viruses and companies have responded with antivirus programs to stop them. The cycle just keeps repeating.

Y2K Bug

YOU KNOW HOW YOUR TEACHER ALWAYS SAID NOT TO CUT CORNERS? IF COMPUTER PROGRAMMERS HAD LISTENED, THE "Y2K BUG" SCARE MIGHT NEVER HAVE HAPPENED.

Without getting too technical or needing a call center, here's the basic problem. When computers were still new, the people programming them used only two digits to represent a year when writing code, because nobody had any idea how long the systems were going to last. So, in coding shortcuts, 1978 became 78, 1992 became 92, and so on.

Makes sense, right? Unfortunately, it turned out a lot of those computers were still going to be around when the calendar switched from 1999 to 2000. And nobody was completely sure what would happen then. By the 1980s, the coming numerical crisis was a big discussion topic for early Internet nerds, and programmers worked to fix the mistake with newer software and hardware.

WHY THE FEAR? Without an update, experts feared, those systems would either crash or start acting like it was 1900 instead of 2000. Naturally, the unfixed "legacy" computers were being used by banks, governments, and other important institutions. Think about your bank accidentally giving you an extra century of interest on your savings account—or your credit card hitting you with late fees going back to the McKinley administration. Or, say, a nuclear missile site getting its schedule thrown out of whack and accidentally launching an attack. As fears of what could happen multiplied, there were news reports of people hoarding food and water in makeshift shelters, or phone and tech companies publicly urging their customers to expect service interruptions in the first hours of the new year.

THE Y2K BUG INSPIRED A BUNCH OF BOOKS ABOUT HOW TO COPE. THE WEIRDEST WAS PROBABLY THE *Y2K SURVIVAL GUIDE AND COOKBOOK*, WHICH INCLUDED RECIPES FOR THOSE HOLED UP IN BUNKERS WITHOUT A REFRIGERATOR OR STOVE.

Figuring that kind of chaos might be a bit of a bad thing, governments and private companies spent massive amounts of cash getting their computers up to speed. Depending on which estimate you believe, the total cost added up to somewhere between $300 billion and $600 billion. All that cost did have a benefit, though, as most computers were successfully fixed long before the New Year's ball dropped in Times Square. The biggest problem that night came at a Japanese nuclear power plant, where radiation detectors failed but nobody was placed at risk. All the Y2K hype did create one never-resolved question—was the relative calm a result of all that intense preparation, or was the threat just completely blown out of proportion?

Cell Phones and Cancer

LOCATION: *Global* | TIME FRAME: *2000s*

FOR EVERY ANNOYING BLABBERMOUTH WHO CAN'T HANG UP THE CELL PHONE EVEN WHILE IN LINE AT THE STORE, THERE ARE DOZENS OF PEOPLE WISHING SOMETHING BAD WOULD HAPPEN TO THAT NUISANCE. AND SOME PEOPLE THINK SOMETHING HORRIBLE WILL.

More than four billion people now use mobile phones. So if there *is* a connection between cell-phone use and cancer, that's a potential health disaster of global proportions. As for the question of whether a connection exists, the answers are at best inconclusive, which has done little to calm fears that holding the phone can have serious side effects.

The reason for the fears? Cell phones give off radio waves, and because people usually keep the phone right against their head during calls, the head absorbs some of those waves. Because people adopted the cell phone so quickly—think about how few people you know had one in

> ❋
>
> THOSE WHO REMAIN CONCERNED ABOUT A CANCER RISK FROM CELL PHONES SHOULD USE AN EARPIECE, BECAUSE IT DOES KEEP THE SOURCE OF THE RADIATION AWAY FROM THE HEAD. THOUGH IT DOES NOTHING TO STOP YOU FROM LOOKING LIKE A CYBORG.
>
> ❋

1998—the technology grew and changed much faster than governments were able to test whether or not it was safe. And in newer phones, the antenna—which draws the largest amount of radiation—was usually inside the phone itself. All of which led to worries that so much close-range radiation could cause various ailments, with brain tumors among the most serious.

WIRELESS INTERNET ALSO PRODUCES ITS OWN ELECTROMAGNETIC FIELD. LUCKILY WI-FI DOESN'T EMIT NEARLY THE LEVELS OF CONCENTRATED RADIATION THAT MOBILE PHONES DO. IN A 2007 STUDY, THE UK'S HEALTH PROTECTION AGENCY FOUND THAT SOMEONE SITTING FOR AN ENTIRE YEAR IN A WI-FI HOT SPOT WOULD COME INTO CONTACT WITH THE SAME AMOUNT OF RADIO WAVES AS IF THEY MADE A MERE TWENTY-MINUTE CELL-PHONE CALL. SO SURF FREELY.

Since 2000, researchers from a number of countries—Sweden, Great Britain, Germany, Denmark, Australia—have conducted studies on the effects of long-term cell-phone use. The good news is the vast majority of them found no evidence to support the link (only one Swedish study deemed inconclusive found an increased risk of a specific type of tumor). The biggest and most frequently cited study, a thirteen-country survey by the INTERPHONE project, found no risk at all, and the National Cancer Institute within the U.S. National Institutes of Health summarizes all research as finding no risk.

THE AFTERMATH While it's probably smart to take commonsense precautions to limit cell-phone use in case new research proves otherwise, it appears there's no definite link to cancer. So much for hoping that the annoying guy yammering about his sex life on the train gets some medical payback.

Chapter 7

Beyond-Our-Control Panics

SOME PANICS REALLY AREN'T WORTH WORRYING ABOUT. Most of these doomsday predictions probably aren't going to come true, and the ones that are probably won't happen in your lifetime. As for the others, there's nothing we can do about them anyway. If a massive earthquake strikes, all people can do is help with the aftermath. In the unlikely event that aliens actually visit Earth, they're obviously way ahead of us. And if a massive asteroid hits us or the fears about 2012 prove correct, the world and most of its life-forms (including us) are going to be goners anyway. So, honestly, don't waste your time worrying about these beyond-our-control potential crises.

Roswell UFO Crash

LOCATION: *United States* | TIME FRAME: *1947–Present*

PERHAPS THE MOST AMAZING THING ABOUT THE "ROSWELL INCIDENT" IS HOW IT TOOK DECADES FOR A SEEMINGLY FORGOTTEN CRASH TO BECOME PROOF OF ALIEN LIFE AND OF A MASSIVE COVER-UP (AT LEAST IN THE MINDS OF CONSPIRACY THEORISTS).

Nobody disputes that on July 8, 1947, an aircraft of some kind crashed on a ranch near Roswell, New Mexico. Personnel responding from the Roswell Army Air Field collected pieces of what was initially described as a "flying disc" and took the debris to a military facility in Fort Worth. There was some confusion about the incident the next day, as one Roswell paper called the object a "flying saucer" and Air Force spokesmen described it as a weather balloon with a radar reflector attached.

So the story stood for more than thirty years. Until 1978, when author Stanton Friedman interviewed a witness from the 1947

> ROSWELL HAS BECOME A GO-TO REFERENCE FOR SCIENCE FICTION, REFERENCED IN EVERYTHING FROM *STAR TREK* AND *DR. WHO* TO *FUTURAMA*. THE FOO FIGHTERS, FRONTED BY UFO FAN DAVE GROHL, NAMED THEIR LABEL ROSWELL RECORDS, AND SKATEBOARDER TONY HAWK INCLUDED A ROSWELL LEVEL IN HIS POPULAR *PRO SKATER* VIDEO GAME.

incident who claimed the crashed object was an alien craft, and theories about the crash started flowing. Americans love a vague conspiracy theory, and soon Roswell books became a cottage industry with accusations of witness intimidation, efforts to copy alien technology, and even an alien autopsy (with widely circulated but obviously fake photos).

WHY THE PANIC? At some point, the Roswell conspiracy theory got folded into conspiracy theories surrounding Area 51, a military base in southern Nevada. Area 51 had been active since at least 1967, mostly concerned with testing new aircraft and weapons systems. The intense secrecy around the base, however, made it easy for conspiracy theorists to claim the supersecret technology the supersecret base was working on had supersecret alien connections. A few former employees claimed to work on captured spacecraft, and the military's refusal to explain the true nature of its projects fit easily into the conspiracy narrative.

THE TOWN OF ROSWELL KNOWS WHERE ITS BREAD IS BUTTERED. EACH JULY 4 WEEKEND IT HOSTS A "UFO FESTIVAL," COMPLETE WITH AN ALIEN-COSTUME CONTEST FOR PETS AND A "GALACTIC MARKETPLACE" SELLING ALIEN-THEMED SWAG.

The wild rumors had enough staying power that, in the 1990s, Congress actually launched an investigation into the Roswell incident. The resulting report found the 1947 crash was part of the then-secret Project Mogul, a clandestine program to develop balloons that could fly over the USSR at high altitude and detect signs of nuclear test sites. The same report blamed eyewitness accounts of alien bodies in the craft on damaged and disfigured test dummies used in the balloon project. Naturally, the congressional report did nothing to satisfy conspiracy theorists; they simply saw it as another step in a government cover-up.

Alien Abduction Stories

LOCATION: *Global* | TIME FRAME: *1957–present*

THE IDEA OF ALIENS ABDUCTING—AND OFTEN UNCOMFORTABLY PROBING— HUMAN BEINGS HAS SPAWNED PLENTY OF SCIENCE FICTION AND COUNTLESS PARODIES. BUT THERE ARE LITERALLY THOUSANDS OF PEOPLE WHO THINK THEY'VE HAD ONE OF THESE TOO-CLOSE ENCOUNTERS.

Nobody knows for sure when the first alien abduction story started making the rounds, but the first to get widespread attention (allegedly) happened in 1957. Brazilian farmer Antonio Villas Boas claimed he was plowing his fields on an October night when he saw a spacecraft approach and land near him. He tried to flee, but was caught by a helmeted being and taken aboard the ship. Once inside, he claimed he was experimented upon by—oh, and made to have sex with—what he considered a particularly attractive alien being.

The first highly publicized American case of alien abduction was reported in 1961, involving Betty and Barney Hill of New Hampshire. The couple claimed to have seen a UFO with humanoid aliens inside while driving down an empty highway. When the UFO got close, the Hills reported seeing bright lights, hearing loud noises, and entering an altered state of consciousness. (No, they were not on drugs.) When they got home, neither could remember a long stretch of their drive home, but both claimed to notice things they couldn't explain, with Betty seeing a weird powder on her dress and Barney feeling a weirder compulsion to keep checking his genitals for . . . something. Betty reported the incident to the Air Force, and soon began having vivid nightmares about her and Barney being examined separately by aliens aboard a ship.

The Hills first discussed their "encounter" publicly at a church meeting more than a year after the incident. Both agreed to undergo hypnosis, and told the hypnotist about their alien probings in detail. While the couple initially tried to avoid publicity, the Hills' hypnosis sessions became international news, and their story wound up inspiring a book and a TV movie.

ASTRONOMER CARL SAGAN (AND OTHERS) THOUGHT ALIEN ABDUCTION STORIES FIT A BIGGER TREND. IN HIS BOOK *THE DEMON-HAUNTED WORLD*, SAGAN WROTE ABOUT HOW PEOPLE AS FAR BACK AS MEDIEVAL TIMES TOLD ODDLY SIMILAR STORIES OF ABDUCTIONS AND EXPERIMENTATION BY VARIOUS DEMONS, FROM SATAN HIMSELF TO THE SEXUALLY AGGRESSIVE SUCCUBUS AND INCUBUS.

WHY THE PANIC? Not surprisingly, it also inspired others to report any number of wild alien adventures. A 1991 study interviewed about six thousand Americans who claimed to have been abducted, and by the mid-1980s, support groups for the abducted were popping up. Researchers who study these abductions—and there are such people—have found a pretty consistent pattern in most abductees' stories. That pattern? A weird feeling pre-abduction, a series of invasive exams aboard the ship, no memory of time while on board, and a "realization event" that makes the victim remember the abduction. Other common stories involve touring the aliens' ship or conversing with the visitors. Some tales have included warnings from the aliens about nuclear weapons, environmental destruction, or other potential calamities. Few anecdotes ever explain the reason for all the invasive physical exams.

While some were obvious hoaxes by attention seekers, in most cases, the "abducted" subjects seem to genuinely believe their accounts really happened. Barring the possibility that spacemen obsessed with human anatomy are actually dropping by, scientists have a few possible explanations for all these similar stories, including post-traumatic stress disorder and sleep deprivation. Whatever the explanation(s), the truth is out there. Just check your watch—and your nether regions—if you ever see anything that looks like a UFO.

> LIFE MIGHT HAVE IMITATED ART TOO CLOSELY FOR AUTHOR LOUIS WHITLEY STRIEBER. ALREADY A SUCCESSFUL HORROR AND FANTASY WRITER, BEST KNOWN FOR *THE HUNGER*, HE CLAIMED TO HAVE BEEN ABDUCTED FROM HIS CABIN BY "VISITORS" IN 1985. HE LATER WROTE THREE "AUTOBIOGRAPHICAL" BOOKS ABOUT THE ALLEGED EXPERIENCE, AS WELL AS SEVERAL NOVELS THAT FEATURED UFOS OR ALIEN ABDUCTIONS.

New Madrid Earthquake

LOCATION: *United States* | TIME FRAME: *December 3, 1990*

DECEMBER 3, 1990, WAS A DAY THE EARTH STOOD STILL. FOR WHICH MANY, MANY SPOOKED MIDWESTERNERS BREATHED A COLLECTIVE SIGH OF RELIEF.

That was the date on which climatologist Iben Browning predicted a 50/50 chance of a catastrophic earthquake along the New Madrid fault line. The New Madrid fault runs through five states, from southern Illinois to northeastern Arkansas, meaning metro areas like Memphis, St. Louis, and potentially Chicago would suffer from such a major quake. Several prominent geologists immediately dismissed Browning's prediction of a 6.5-magnitude quake, pointing out that (among other things) Browning was a climatologist, not a geologist, and that there was no scientific basis for such a quake happening.

However, Browning made his prediction in November 1989, just a few weeks after the Loma Prieta quake rocked San Francisco

> THE NEW MADRID FAULT HAS A DESTRUCTIVE HISTORY. THE 1811–1812 NEW MADRID QUAKES WERE THE LARGEST EVER RECORDED IN AMERICA— MORE THAN FORTY TIMES AS POWERFUL AS THE 1906 EARTHQUAKE THAT LEVELED SAN FRANCISCO. ONE EVEN CAUSED THE MISSISSIPPI RIVER TO RUN BACKWARD FOR A FEW HOURS.

and killed fifty-seven people. Some news articles credited Browning with using his theories of tidal stress causing seismic activity to correctly predict that quake (as well as the 1980 eruption of Mount Saint Helens). The coverage of Browning's forecast and the debate over said forecast managed to scare a lot of people. The main paper in Memphis even started running a daily "Quake Watch" while consistently pointing out that the evidence didn't support the fear. Sales of earthquake insurance spiked, a handful of schools in four different states closed for a few days around December 3, and there were reports of people fleeing their homes in case the quake hit.

> WHEN IT CAME TO PREDICTIONS, BROWNING HAD NOTHING ON TECUMSEH. WHILE HEADING TO DETROIT TO ROUND UP ALLIES FOR A COMING BATTLE IN 1811, THE SHAWNEE LEADER TOLD A CREEK CHIEF, "WHEN I ARRIVE THERE, I WILL STAMP ON THE GROUND WITH MY FOOT, AND SHAKE DOWN EVERY HOUSE IN TUCKHABATCHEE." ON THE EXACT DAY HE ARRIVED IN DETROIT, A MASSIVE QUAKE HIT THE NEW MADRID FAULT. NOW, *THAT'S* A PREDICTION.

THE AFTERMATH Of course, the deadline passed without even a tremor. When Browning died a mere seven months after his prediction proved a dud, he was better known for that error than anything else in his scientific career. But he was right about the potential of the New Madrid fault line—eighteen years later, on April 18, 2008, a quake measuring 5.2 on the Richter scale did unexpectedly hit in southern Illinois. (Luckily, it caused minimal damage.) So one could argue Browning's prediction sort of came true—albeit a mere 6,346 days too late.

End of the World

LOCATION: *Global* | TIME FRAME: *December 21, 2012*

IF YOU'RE READING THIS PAGE AFTER DECEMBER 21, 2012, THEN NONE OF IT REALLY MATTERS. HOWEVER, THANKS TO A BIZARRE COMBINATION OF MODERN ASTRONOMY AND THE ASTROLOGY OF THE ANCIENT MAYANS (SERIOUSLY), THERE'S A SMALL SEGMENT OF THE POPULATION THAT RECKONS THAT'LL BE THE DAY OF THE FINAL RECKONING. IF THEY'RE RIGHT, YOU'RE PROBABLY TOO BUSY LEADING A BAND OF SURVIVORS IN A POSTAPOCALYPTIC NIGHTMARE TO BOTHER WITH THIS.

It all starts with the Mesoamerican "Long Count" calendar the Mayans helped popularize. Unlike a mere annual calendar (the Mayans had one of those, too), the Long Count was used to measure periods of more than fifty-two years. Its creators understood the moon, sun, and planets so well that they predicted eclipses, lunar cycles—everything but winning lottery numbers—centuries ahead of time with amazing accuracy.

MOST 2012 THEORISTS ARE PRETTY VAGUE ON WHAT THEY THINK WILL ACTUALLY *HAPPEN* ON THAT DAY. ONE EXCEPTION IS "POLAR SHIFT"—A PSEUDOSCIENTIFIC THEORY THAT CLAIMS THE UNUSUAL SUN-GALAXY ALIGNMENT COULD CHANGE EARTH'S MAGNETIC FIELD AND SHIFT ITS AXIS. THAT MEANS DIFFERENT SPOTS ON THE GLOBE WOULD BECOME THE NORTH AND SOUTH POLES, KILLING ANYTHING UNABLE TO QUICKLY ADAPT TO ITS NEW CLIMATE.

That perfect track record is pretty freaky—freaky enough to spark doomsday predictions. Experts on the Mayans somehow figured out that the calendar started on August 13 of the year 3114 BCE. Now, here's the thing. The calendar is divided into eras lasting 5,126 years each. The current era ends (drumroll, please) on December 21, 2012. Because our current era is also the last one detailed in the Long Count, the doomsayers figure the calendar treats 12/21/12 as the end of not just an era, but of life on Earth.

LOOK AT IT THIS WAY—2012 ISN'T THE FIRST DATE PEOPLE THOUGHT THE WORLD WOULD END. IN THE FINAL YEARS OF THE TWENTIETH CENTURY, BELIEVERS IN THE SO-CALLED BETHLEHEM PROPHECIES (ALLEGED LOST TEXTS) AND "THE BIBLE CODE" (HIDDEN MESSAGES IN THE OLD TESTAMENT) GENUINELY THOUGHT THE START OF THE NEW MILLENNIUM WOULD BE THE END OF THE WORLD. SOME EVEN SOLD ALL THEIR STUFF, WHICH THEY PROBABLY REGRETTED ON JANUARY 1, 2000.

WHY THE PANIC? Adding fuel to the fire, scientists have pointed out that on that date, the sun will align with the center of the Milky Way galaxy for the first time in, oh, nearly twenty-six thousand years. The end-of-the-world crowd claim to have found evidence of that crucial date in the Chinese *I Ching*, the Bible, ancient Greek prophecies, and the always-popular Nostradamus.

What does it all mean? Neither the ancient Mayans nor recent astronomers knew what specific impact, if any, the unusual astronomical alignment on 12/21/12 would have. The date just marks the end of one Mayan time period and the start of another, and humanity has already survived several eras in the calendar's math. Just to be safe, the first 2012 disaster movie jumped the gun and hit theaters in 2009.

Asteroid Colliding with the Earth

LOCATION: *Global* | TIME FRAME: *Future*

IT SOUNDS LIKE THE PLOT OF A BAD JERRY BRUCKHEIMER MOVIE—COME TO THINK OF IT, IT *HAS* BEEN THE PLOT OF A BAD JERRY BRUCKHEIMER MOVIE. BUT A GIANT ASTEROID OR METEORITE COLLIDING WITH THE EARTH IS AMONG THE MOST LIKELY SCENARIOS FOR WHAT WILL EVENTUALLY DESTROY THE WORLD—AND NOT EVEN BRUCE WILLIS CAN SAVE US.

More than a thousand asteroids at least a mile in length pass near our planet, with an eighteen-mile-wide asteroid the largest discovered so far. To put it mildly, anything that big hitting the earth would be bad.

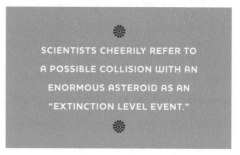

SCIENTISTS CHEERILY REFER TO A POSSIBLE COLLISION WITH AN ENORMOUS ASTEROID AS AN "EXTINCTION LEVEL EVENT."

The collision alone would wipe out everyone near the impact site, but that's the least of it. An impact that big would set off a chain reaction of all kinds of seismic activity, including volcanoes, earthquakes, and tsunamis. If that's not bad enough, all the earth and dust kicked up by the geological chaos would fill the sky, blocking sunlight from getting through the atmosphere. Without sun, all plant life would die. Any surviving animals, including people, wouldn't survive long without plants.

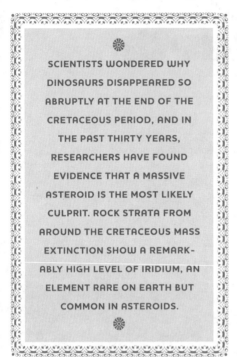

SCIENTISTS WONDERED WHY DINOSAURS DISAPPEARED SO ABRUPTLY AT THE END OF THE CRETACEOUS PERIOD, AND IN THE PAST THIRTY YEARS, RESEARCHERS HAVE FOUND EVIDENCE THAT A MASSIVE ASTEROID IS THE MOST LIKELY CULPRIT. ROCK STRATA FROM AROUND THE CRETACEOUS MASS EXTINCTION SHOW A REMARK-ABLY HIGH LEVEL OF IRIDIUM, AN ELEMENT RARE ON EARTH BUT COMMON IN ASTEROIDS.

WHY THE PANIC? Smaller asteroids and meteorites actually hit the earth pretty regularly. The planet's surface is dotted with craters from impacts throughout history and prehistory. The worst recent collision, the 1908 Tunguska event in Siberia, caused a large explosion that reportedly leveled forests for more than eighty miles. Other explosions occur at altitudes too high to do major damage, though their resulting fireballs can be seen from the ground—with the most recent example being a January 2008 fireball above the Canadian Yukon.

Impacts are a serious enough threat that NASA has a Near Earth Object Program tasked with tracking any comets, meteors, and asteroids that come close to our planet. The NEOP maintains a Web site listing all the objects expected to hit Earth in the next hundred years, so if the big one comes, at least we'll probably know about it first.

Index

About the Author

JEFF FLEISCHER is a Chicago-based journalist and author. He has worked as an editorial fellow at *Mother Jones,* a reporter in residence at the *Sydney Morning Herald,* an Alicia Patterson Foundation reporting fellow, and the national politics and op/ed editor for *University Wire.* He has contributed to *The New Republic, National Geographic Traveler's Intelligent Travel, Chicago Magazine, Mental_Floss, BuzzFlash, The Daily Herald, World Jewish Digest, Women's eNews, Rugby Magazine, Chicago Wilderness, The Chicago Reader,* the *Southland (New Zealand) Times* and numerous other publications, with his work appearing in more than 30 countries on every continent but Antarctica. He has a master's from Northwestern University's Medill School of Journalism and a bachelor's in journalism and history from Indiana University. For more information, visit www.JeffFleischer.com